Blooming

This Pilgrim's Progress

Marian den Boer

BLOOMING: THIS PILGRIM'S PROGRESS
Copyright © 2009 Marian den Boer

All rights reserved.

ISBN-10: 1-897373-65-1
ISBN-13: 978-1-897373-65-1

All rights reserved. No part of this publication may be reproduced, stored in a retrieval system, or transmitted in any form or by any means—electronic, mechanical, photocopying, recording, or any other—except for brief quotations in printed reviews, without the prior written consent of the copyright owner or publisher. Any unauthorized publication is an infringement of the copyright law.

Unless otherwise indicated, Scripture has been taken from the HOLY BIBLE, NEW INTERNATIONAL VERSION®. Copyright © 1973, 1978, 1984 by International Bible Society. Used by permission of Zondervan Bible Publishers. All rights reserved.

Published by Word Alive Press

131 Cordite Road, Winnipeg, Manitoba, R3W 1S1
www.wordalivepress.ca

To my brothers
Bill, Al, Larry, Mike, John

Philippians 3:9–14

Acknowledgements

Thank you to my family who let me write about them.

Thanks to Joan Marshall and Keith Carroll who showed me what this book was about and helped me get it into shape.

Thanks to Bert Witvoet and Marian Van Til at the *Christian Courier* where many of these "slices" were originally published.

But most of all, thanks to God,

> *I lift up my eyes to you, to you whose throne is in heaven. (Psalm 123:1)*

Table of Contents

Acknowledgements   v

Introduction   xi

Old Testimony   1

1. Don't wreck the flowers   3
2. Calling a plumber   6
3. A war of wills among the lilacs   9
4. Model Children   12
5. Life in the big city   15
6. Back to work   18
7. Going downhill   20
8. Shamed by the Dust   23
9. Alone at the helm   26
10. Be careful what you pray   30
11. Bird watching   33
12. Gift from dad   35
13. We all have different talents   38
14. Food for thought   41
15. The gift that wasn't   44
16. A 40-day experience   47
17. The 'old' Dutch mother   49
18. A greasy situation   51
19. Sin and anger   53
20. The prodigal   55
21. Life with a dog   58
22. A Sunday morning alternative   61
23. Not like the good old days   64
24. A 'short stay'   67
25. A master thief   70
26. Crime on our street   72

27. On becoming 40	75
28. A prayer with instant answers	77
29. Ants	79
30. A story of Rachel and Leah	81
31. A good deed, indeed!	84
32. More precious than gold	86
33. A thorn in the side	88
34. Tough love	90
35. Spring and cleaning	92
36. Training my children	94
37. A life-changing challenge	96
38. I blush to tell you this	98
39. A pig and a whistle	100
40. A fake fireplace	103
41. Curing an irritating habit	106
42. Things are never what they seem	108
43. To soar like an eagle	111
44. Loving your neighbours	114
45. The most delicious ice-cream sundae imaginable	117
46. I Love You, Dad	119
47. The reluctant fisher-woman	121
48. How does one deal with death? With life?	123
49. Genetic Tears	125
50. Secrets of a driving instructor	128
51. Now that my husband is my boss...	131
52. My pastor's sermon changed my life	133

New Testimony 136

53. Psalm 51 as it happened to me	137
54. It just never got warm	139
55. The parable of the pool	141
56. The automatic garage-door opener	143
57. A storm in the living room	145
58. Out of love for my husband	147
59. She loves me	149
60. Losing my licence	151
61. The Culprit	153

62. Cleaning Up	156
63. The Lightning of God	158
64. Saved by Grace	160
65. We had our infants baptized or did we?	162
66. Grounded in Christ	164
67. Flying High	166
68. Mission-Trip Blues	168
69. This is the Day the Lord Has Made or A Day in the Life of a Homemaker	170
70. Absence Makes the Heart Grow Fonder	172
71. The Parable of the Window Seat	174
72. The Parable of the Direction Sheet	176
73. The Parable of the Firemen	178
74. The Parable of the Membership Card	180
75. Fly the Cat and Making Sacrifices	182
76. A Dogma Dies	184
77. Enough Already!	186
78. Cooking in Faith	189
79. That Still Small Voice	191
80. Where is the Life Jacket?	193
81. The Heads of the House	196
82. Football Foul-up	199
83. Telephone Trap	202
84. Cat	204
85. The Conversion of Mrs. Z.	207
86. My Treasures?	210
87. A Spotless Bride	212

Introduction

My friend Dini and I had at least 78 years of wall-papering know-how between us, so when the church was looking for volunteers to paper the master bedroom during the parsonage makeover project, that job had Dini and Marian written all over it.

When we showed up at 10 o'clock on Thursday morning, the walls of the unfurnished room had been sized, according to Dini's request, and numerous wall-papering gadgets were at our disposal: two plastic smoothers, a measuring tape, a laser level for checking the plumb line, a flimsy plastic wallpaper tray, three useless card tables, a step stool, scissors and a pencil. The pastor's wife showed us the beige with-green-pinstripe wallpaper. It reminded me of one of my husband's old suits.

The paper was very thin. To a less experienced team it could have proved a nightmare, but Dini and I knew exactly how to work with it. We measured, cut, and hung that room in less than four hours. Every piece lined up perfectly. We flowed, thanking the Lord at every corner. We would have trimmed the top and bottom edges as well, but the thin damp paper was prone to tear. The pastor's wife agreed to finish up when the paper dried.

The following week at a ladies' social it was rumoured that our paper had fallen off the wall. Mary heard it from the pastor's wife. Of course, she was using the electric sander at the time, so she could have heard wrong. Tami, though, had seen the room. There was no paper on the wall. It was an unfinished room with blotchy walls. Dini and I were baffled.

Professionals couldn't have done a better, neater job. Never in our combined 78 years of wall-paper know-how had any of our work suffered such consequences. It couldn't be true.

That night I had a revelation. The walls of the bedroom had recently been painted with a latex paint. The paint hadn't had time to cure properly. The paper sucked the water out of the paint, the paint crumbled, so of course, the paper came down.

On Sunday morning the pastor's wife approached wearing a sheepish look. I beat her to the punch. "The paper fell down."

"You're asking me if the paper fell down?"

"No, I'm telling you the paper fell down."

"It didn't fall down. I took it down."

Right then, I could have "took" her down, but we were in church....

No, that was the old me. The "being-transformed" me quietly questioned, *Lord, what is this about? Surely, Dini and I didn't spend four hours enjoying each other's company, hanging paper perfectly just to have it torn down?*

The pastor's wife explained the stripes were dizzying and served to emphasize every bump and jag already clearly defined by the very thin paper. The pastor's wife didn't like it, so she took it down.

At the beginning of this book I had my life papered neatly in straight lines. My Christianity lined up. I hung it myself with the help of my friends, my Bible studies, my private devotions, my mealtime rituals, my church attendance and my acts of charity. One could see the imperfections in my self-righteous life somewhat highlighted by the Ten Commandments, but heaven would fix that.

Well, although the undercoat was good God didn't like the choice of paper. He took it down and He's replacing it with the righteousness of His Son—thicker, richly textured wallpaper that covers the flaws perfectly. At the top edge He plans to hang a border of blooming lilies.

The stories in this book reveal the day-to-day experiences of my sometimes frazzled self as I mothered six children over a period of approximately 15 years. The Holy Spirit subtly, yet dramatically, convicted and convinced me in the nitty gritty of everyday family life.

Most of the stories in this book were originally written for a "Slice of Bread" column in a Christian tabloid, *The Christian Courier*. Scripture verses and spiritual applications have been added for the purposes of this book. In writing the columns I simply wanted to entertain others by sharing what was happening in our household.

When I began recording the stories, Marty and I had been married for nine years and were the parents of four children: Angela (7), Allison (5), Paul (3) and Michelle (1). I lived Christianity from my head. As the years progressed God patiently changed me into someone who attempts to live Christianity from the heart as led by His Spirit. *My sheep listen to my voice; I know them, and they follow me. (John 10:27)*

Marian den Boer, December 2008

Old Testimony

He made me look
inside my heart,
so I could part
with every rotten thing
that was my king
instead of Him.

Don't Wreck the Flowers

In the fall of 1987 our family of six moved into a run-down house in a kept-up neighbourhood. Whether looking indoors, outdoors or at the doors, we could see home-improvement projects.

Every project tackled, sprouted another: we painted the walls and suddenly the floor appeared unbearably ugly; we fixed a leaky faucet and discovered the counter top had rotted beyond repair; we pulled the tattered carpet off the front steps and the glue remained.

At our previous homes, the first warm spring evening would find Marty and me strolling in the park, or lounging on the deck or under a maple tree sipping our evening coffee, listening to the birds.

However, early on this first warm spring evening while our children and at least eight others rode up and down the street on bicycles, tricycles and roller skates, Marty and I attacked the house. I chose to tackle the carpet glue on the front porch with varnish remover and a scraper. Marty decided this was the evening to take down the ragged awning above the large bay window off the living room.

Directly below this twenty-pane window was a lovely recently hoed flowerbed alive with dozens of red tulips, scatters of blue forget-me-nots, and promises of peonies, roses and assorted border perennials. This flowerbed was probably the most attractive feature of the house.

"Don't wreck any flowers," I warned as Marty looked for a place to plant his stepladder. Heedfully he set the ladder's feet at the outer edge of the flowerbed, so that the ladder stretched over the lovely blooms and rested neatly against the tube frame of the awning. Armed with a vise-grip, he climbed to the third step from the top, from where he could reach over the rolled-up awning to unscrew the canvas from the house.

As he twisted his vise-grip against the second rusted wing-nut, he could feel the ladder sink until it was no longer leaning against the awning frame. Marty jumped clear sending the ladder crashing into the window. The sound of shattering glass echoed around us. Marty looked furtively about expecting to see neighbours popping from doors and windows, but fortunately the children were playing with such exuberance, not even they noticed the noise of the crash.

At this point I told myself to keep quiet (a lesson learned early in our marriage). It is better to bite and injure my tongue than to talk during accidents or disasters involving my spouse. I scraped vigorously at the steps. Marty looked sheepish. He got a bucket and tossed in bits of glass from the two broken panes as well as the red heads of three decapitated tulips.

It dawned on me my concern for the flowerbed had blinded me to the real hazards of the job. I rethought my priorities. What is easier to repair or replace: a few flowers, a window, or a husband?

As Marty remounted the ladder now firmly planted among the tulip stems, I voiced my concern.

"Don't hurt yourself, dear!"

"Oh shut up," he replied. Then he grinned.

The rest of the job went rather smoothly.

> *"Woe to you, teachers of the law and Pharisees, you hypocrites! You are like whitewashed tombs, which look beautiful on the outside but on the inside are full of dead men's bones and everything unclean. In the same way, on the outside you appear to people as righteous but on the inside you are full of hypocrisy and wickedness."*
> *(Matthew 23:27–28)*

I saw beauty in the religious flowerbeds of my life. I boasted that our new home was within blocks of our church and the Christian school. My day was not complete without Bible reading and prayer after every meal—it didn't matter that I usually daydreamed during devotions (I didn't usually notice my tulips either as I rushed in and out of my home). And, just as I was oblivious to the precarious situation in which my husband put himself to honour my request concerning the flowers, I didn't often consider Jesus as I kept this lovely religious life in order.

Calling a Plumber

One morning I discovered a dripping pipe under my kitchen sink.

What to do? I had three choices: call a plumber, tell my husband or fix it myself. A plumber would mean money, my husband was at the office, so I decided to fix it myself.

It looked like a simple matter; tighten the pipe. I grabbed a vise-grip and gave the pipe a twist. Water sprayed out in every direction.

Back to option two; I phoned Marty.

"Where in the basement is the main valve to our water?"

"Why?"

I watched my kitchen becoming a pool.

Husbands don't always insist on knowing all the details; only when they know you would rather not tell. After he had been completely informed, Marty told me where to look.

I found the valve, turned off the water and got my mop.

Two hours later I was ready for my first option: call a plumber. I turned to "Plumbing" in the yellow pages. A big clean ad for *C. Hook and Son* grabbed my attention. A nice family business, I thought. I dialled the number. A secretary answered. Her expensive professional voice should have been my hint as to the overhead involved with this company.

Minutes later a brand new, brightly painted plumber's van pulled into the driveway. A middle-aged fellow in a stunning uniform handed me his gold-embossed business card. I led him to the kitchen, sketching the details (I left out the part about the vise-grip).

He stationed me at the main valve in the basement and took his place under the sink. Every few minutes he yelled, "Off" or "On" and shortly "Okay, I got it."

"Well," he said, "that takes care of 90 per cent of your problem."

"Now we're back to where I was before the vise-grip," I thought. I wondered how he was going to fix my original problem.

He fed it to me a little at a time. First he told me, this leak had been going on a long time, probably a year. "How long have you lived here?"

I was relieved to be able to say, "Only a few months." Then he told me all about how people don't know what to look for when they buy a house.

I let him know we had checked under the sink and noticed the brand new plastic drain pipes.

"That Mickey Mouse garbage," he sneered. "Some joker didn't know what he was doing."

I tried to gain some esteem, "Well, we got the house cheaper because it needed work."

"That's the way to do it," he admitted.

Encouraged, I went on, "Eventually we want to replace all these cupboards." I was thinking years; he was thinking weeks. "You might as well order them now," he said. Then he gave me the lowdown.

"Your faucets are worn out. They've been leakin' so long your counter top's all rotted out. You need a whole new counter top. Put new faucets on this old rotted top and you'll end up with the whole works fallin' through to the basement. You might as well get the cupboards at the same time. Your sink is pretty old too. Let us know when you get the stuff installed and I'll connect the pipes up for you."

"Of course," he added gently, "I'll have to charge you for the work I did today." I think he guessed about the vise-grip.

He sat down at the kitchen table with his bill book. He thought, and then scribbled an amount.

I gasped when he handed me a bill for $69.63. I looked at the clock; he'd only been in my home 15 minutes. He hadn't used any parts and I'd done some of his labour.

To cheer me up, he told me how wonderful water was and he let me in on a marvellous get-rich-quick scheme: if I tossed a coin in a dish every time I turned on the tap, very soon I'd have enough for a nice trip to Florida. "Try it!" he challenged.

> *"Go and tell Hezekiah, 'This is what the Lord, the God of your father David, says: I have heard your prayer and seen your tears; I will add fifteen years to your life.'"* (Isaiah 38:5)

I attacked those pipes without knowing much about plumbing. I saw the result of my misguided efforts almost immediately as water squirted in all directions.

This is a picture of my spiritual efforts. Too often I pray without considering possible consequences of an answered prayer. Nor do I consider if my request lines up with the Lord's will. What are the results of those prayers? Does God account for my ignorance and make adjustments? Does He simply say "no," for my own good, or does He say "yes" as He did to King Hezekiah even though the Lord knew the mess the good king was about to make?

A War of Wills Among the Lilacs

When we were first married Marty tried his dad's style of running a household. This made me livid. His father and mother had their world divided into his domain, her domain and a mutual domain where he had the final say.

I balked when Marty tried to adopt some of his parents' domain procedures. In their scheme of things the kitchen, cooking, cleaning and shopping belonged absolutely to the woman; the garage, the lawn, household maintenance and repair belonged to the man. The woman needed never lift a hammer or a screwdriver and the man could be entirely ignorant of how to boil water or make an ice cube.

This worked excellently for people who happily agreed to run their routine that way, but when Marty, early in our marriage, according to an example set by his father, looked at me, then at his empty teacup and then at the teapot on the kitchen counter and naively expected a full cup by this procedure, it occurred to me to pour the tea on his head. Overcoming that impulse, I simply mimicked him and asked if he was an invalid.

As a matter of course, we've established our own unspoken routines in the years since: I always peel his oranges, he always makes breakfast, I always take the garbage out, and so on. It's when the two households meet on overnight visits that the differences are spotlighted.

One spring weekend Marty's parents came to spend some time with our family. On Sunday afternoon, we took them to the lilac dell at the Royal Botanical Gardens for Lilac Sunday. On Lilac Sunday, 749 different types of lilacs—the largest collection in the world—are in full fragrant bloom. Garden visitors are invited to stroll down the lovely grassy purple and white valley, seating themselves among the sweet-smelling bushes to enjoy the music of a brass quartet and watch an artist recreate the dell on canvas.

Marty and I thought this would especially delight Marty's mom as she loves both flowers and music. Marty's dad is more interested in history, philosophy, farming, and he likes the shade. Marty enjoys anything outdoors and being with his family. Myself, I find an artist at work fascinating. Our four children usually enjoy an outing and our oldest, Angela, likes to be close to the action.

As we trailed down into the dell toward the musicians, absorbing sights, sounds and smells, Marty's dad pointed toward a large shade tree on a scarcely peopled incline directly behind the action.

Angela whispered to me, "I'd like to be where we can see."

She had voiced my sentiments exactly, but the rest of the family were already well on the way to the shade tree; bypassing the need for a family discussion over such a minor decision.

Letting my rebellious, selfish nature rule, I led Angela further down the slope toward the musicians and the artist. We settled near the front a little to the right of centre. From there we could see the musicians, the painter and the edges of our family arranging themselves on the opposite slope behind a purple lilac bush.

Marty scanned the dell for his wayward wife and child. We waved. He didn't see us; he was looking higher up, further back. The musicians were playing a waltz; on the left an old couple was dancing, her skirt flying and his long gray beard waving as they frolicked; the painter had his canvas covered in several shades of green and was applying dabs of light purple. His painting arm flowed to the music. With the corner of my eye I caught Marty and Allison making their way across the dell. I waved. They were looking in the wrong place.

Again, I became caught up in the motion of the artist. He was applying a darker purple. Suddenly Marty and Allison were with us. "Here you are."

I felt like a child about to be reprimanded. "Look at the artist," I said. "He's painting the dell."

"It's better over here," said Marty. "Allison, go get the others." She ran off; I breathed a sigh of relief.

In a few minutes the whole family was seated around us. I wouldn't look at Marty's parents—I felt too much like a spoilt brat.

Marty said, "It's better here, more comfortable."

His father directed an accusing comment in a bantering tone at me, "But, you didn't follow your husband!" He had to say it twice.

I thought, "You mean, I didn't follow my father-in-law," but I mumbled, "This was just the obvious place to go." The lilacs may have been in full fragrant bloom that day, but I certainly wasn't.

Looking at it now, in a less emotional light, I should have apologized for my disrespectful, selfish action, but I wasn't sorry then and I'm only a wee bit sorry now. I wish we were all in heaven; then this sort of thing wouldn't happen.

But why do we pray, "Thy will be done on earth as it is in heaven," if it isn't possible?

> *Therefore, if anyone is in Christ, he is a new creation; the old has gone, the new has come! (2Corinthians 5:17)*

At this stage in my life, I believed my disrespectful, selfish nature was part of me. I knew I was flawed by sin, but there was absolutely nothing I could do about it this side of heaven, except repent for misdeeds. And if I could justify my transgressions I wouldn't consider repenting. I believed I could expect myself to go on sinning the same selfish rebellious sins until the day I died. Jesus paid for my sin. Yet, it was inconceivable to me that He also could touch the root of my sin and change me.

In the not so distant future I would discover God is the God of the impossible.

Model Children

One Easter Sunday morning Marty had to baby-sit toddlers during the worship service. I didn't envy him until afterward. Our children had been quiet little worshippers of late, which created within me a peaceful assurance of good behaviour as we filed into the pew, second from the front, the same pew we had occupied during the Good Friday service.

Three-year-old Michelle hugged the aisle seat; Paul, 6, claimed the position next to her; Allison, 8, resigned herself to the next spot; while ten-year-old Angela and I tripped past the three of them to the centre of the bench.

"Oh look at the pretty Easter lilies!" I whispered.

"Is that ring of thorns for Jesus' crown of thorns?" asked Angela.

"Yes, it is," I answered sitting back to scan the bulletin.

An elderly gentleman tapped me on the shoulder, "My wife and I sat here behind your family on Good Friday and we think you have model children."

I blushed with pride. "Thank you," I beamed.

"Yes, perfect children!" He patted Allison's head.

Paul's eyes gleamed. Michelle straightened her posture. It didn't occur to me that having my two youngest side by side just beyond my reach might be a problem. I didn't remember that Marty usually anticipated unmanageable arrangements and quietly orchestrated seating.

All went reasonably well until we were standing for the first hymn, "Up, From the Grave He Arose."

Michelle walked along on the pew and stood on tiptoe to reach my ear. "Mommy, pepper," she whispered loudly. She knew I kept a roll of peppermints in my purse.

"Later, after the song."

In a pout, she lay down behind her brother and sister, tapping her shoes repeatedly on the wooden bench.

I bent down to admonish, "No, Michelle."

The tapping stopped and the hymn reclaimed my attention.

> *He tore the bars away. Jesus, my Lord.*
> *Up from the grave He arose, He arose!*
> *With a mighty triumph o'er His foes.*
> *He arose! He arose a Victor from the dark domain,*
> *And He lives forever with His saints to reign.*
> *He arose! He arose!*
> *Hallelujah! Christ arose!*

Then the music stopped and Paul accidentally sat on Michelle who was still sprawled out along the bench. She squealed, scrambling back to her spot.

I reached across and gave her a peppermint. She dropped it. Paul, who doesn't like peppermints, crawled under the bench to retrieve it. Michelle, mistaking his brotherly efforts for theft, exclaimed, "I want it."

I blushed, this time with embarrassment as I imagined the couple behind us shaking their heads, regretting their earlier remarks.

Several long minutes later the minister kindly announced, "The children may now leave for Sunday School."

I sighed with relief as Paul and Michelle skipped out, quarters safely tucked in their little fists, taking with them my fear of further distraction.

On my own way out, I avoided the eyes of the elderly couple behind me. I can honestly say I came home without my sinful pride.

When pride comes, then comes disgrace, but with humility comes wisdom. (Proverbs 11:2)

My darling children sat very still on Good Friday. They became a distraction on Easter Sunday. I felt proud about the impression they made on Friday and was embarrassed on Sunday even though Michelle obeyed when told to stop tapping and Paul sat on his sister purely by accident and had attempted to help her by getting the peppermint. What the people behind me might be thinking was my main concern.

Jesus *made himself nothing, (Philippians 2:7)*. He wasn't influenced by what people thought. His goal was to please the Father. He died to please the Father. That is what Good Friday is about. God wants us to be like Jesus.

Life in the Big City

Under most circumstances I would not pick New York City as the place to spend even part of our family's annual vacation. Holidays are precious. When I think of a vacation, I think of nature: forests, lakes, camping and quiet, slow, peaceful days with the occasional hike, boat trip or lazy afternoon at the beach.

New York City is fast, dirty, noisy, crowded and expensive, but Marty's brother lives there and he's rather likeable, so this fall Marty, Angela and I traded a few, quiet, peaceful, holiday days for life in the fast lane.

The drive from Niagara Falls down through New York State was pleasant enough—very scenic, although Angela found it boring.

Boring changed to frightening once we turned onto the George Washington Bridge. The George Washington Bridge is at least eight lanes wide and two levels deep, filled with cars driven by aggressive New Yorkers.

It cost three dollars to drive into New York over the George Washington Bridge. It cost us six dollars because we had to do it twice. The first time we got into the wrong lane which led to no place on our simple hand-drawn map. Our only recourse was to turn around and begin again.

The second time over the bridge Marty became aggressive, Angela prayed, and I navigated. It worked. We got through Manhattan and into Brooklyn with only one missed turn-off; but by the time we got to Uncle Doug's brownstone, Marty was ready to abandon the car and fly back to quiet peaceful Ontario where drivers acknowledged each other.

Uncle Doug smiled benevolently at our inexperience and proceeded to educate us in the ways and wonders of the big city. Always drive as if you own the streets—never even glance at the other guy. Always lock your car and hide your radio. Ignore panhandlers especially the creative types who offer to watch your car while you are in a restaurant, or to clean your windows at a stoplight, or who need money to buy milk for the baby. They are all drug addicts or alcoholics.

Always count your change. If you are a pedestrian, green means go and red means go faster. If a vehicle hits you, the driver is in the wrong.

For several exciting days we toured the city. We rode the subway, visited the Statue of Liberty, ascended the Empire State Building, bought a toaster in Macy's, saw two undercover police officers making an arrest on Broadway, strolled across the scraggly grass in Central Park, discovered a display of Indian artefacts from British Columbia at the American Museum of Natural History and experienced the Grand Canyon on New York's largest motion picture screen.

On Sunday Doug drove us to a church where, after a service on Christian living, we could buy coffee and cake for 35 cents each. The jangle of silver brought to mind the money changers in the temple. (As good Calvinists we avoided spending money on Sunday. By spending money we would be making someone work for that money. This was against the fourth commandment.)

Did we protest? Well, we mentioned our discomfort to Doug who explained that a decision had been made to make the coffee ministry self-supporting. It sounded perfectly reasonable.

We sipped our coffee as we chatted with a friend of Doug's who suggested we scan the city from the impressive church tower.

We were directed to the Visitor's Center where among the records, tapes, pamphlets and books on sale, we could purchase tower tickets for one dollar each. Uncle Doug bought the tickets.

Did we protest? Who were we to challenge the ways of a big city church? When in Rome do as the Romans. It was truly an impressive tower full of ringing bells.

> *"Not everyone who says to me, 'Lord, Lord,' will enter the kingdom of heaven, but only he who does the will of my Father who is in heaven." (Matthew 7:21)*

I was trying to obey the Ten Commandments and be a good person, but somehow this was not working. Would Jesus write off all the panhandlers as drug addicts and alcoholics, not worth a second glance? Would Jesus avoid buying coffee and cake on Sunday? How did He spend his time when He went to the big city? Who was His guide?

Back to Work

For ten years I'd been a stay-at-home mother, not particularly looking forward to the day when all four children would be in school, setting me free to join the national work force.

Then two years before I planned to begin looking for a job, a perfectly tempting part-time position beckoned, a wonderful caring Christian babysitter for my three-year-old materialized, and the family promised to help on the home front. I went for it.

For the first month, everything was rosy. The babysitter toilet-trained Michelle within a week—something I had been attempting unsuccessfully for over a year. The children took on their extra chores with minimum complaining and Marty maintained a helpful, encouraging attitude.

Then one morning we slept in a few minutes longer than usual. On this particular morning, Allison decided she needed help choosing her clothes, Paul discovered a form to be filled out immediately, and my panty hose ran during breakfast.

After breakfast, we hurried through devotions, Marty started the dishes and I ran down to the freezer for a chicken to pop into the crock pot. When I got the chicken up to the kitchen, I realized it was not a chicken at all, but a bag full of bacon rind shaped like a chicken. I dumped the rind into the garbage and tried again. There are some parts of a quarter pig you don't appreciate as much as others.

The freezer didn't yield a chicken so I quickly chose a package of steak. In the kitchen again, I tugged at the brown paper wrap which was creased and frozen into the meat. The meat hung on. I ran hot water over the package. That did the trick. Once the wrapping had been removed I had two large T-bone steaks with wax paper frozen between them.

Not wanting to cook the paper, I stabbed at the steaks (which were soft at the edges from the hot water treatment) with a long, pointed, serrated knife while firing questions at the kids, "Did you brush your teeth? Comb your hair? Is your school bag packed?"

Suddenly the steaks slipped, and I stabbed directly between the thumb and index finger of my steak-holding hand. Before I felt the pain I jerked the knife out, dropped everything and dashed to the washroom yelling for Marty and calling myself stupid. I ran water over the wound and squeezed it closed without looking. I would have fainted if I had looked. By this time Marty realized I was in trouble.

He examined the gash, gave me a dish towel to wrap my hand and told me to lie down, while he rushed the three school children out the door—Angela and Allison with empathic tears streaming down their cheeks.

As I lay on the living room carpet, groaning to offset the throbbing pain, Marty dumped the steaks into the crock pot, paper and all. Then he drove Michelle to the sitter's.

Flesh wounds (no matter whose) always turn me pale and dizzy. Even as I write this I feel faint....

Suffice it to say, two hours later, I was at work after receiving three stitches, a tetanus shot and some helpful advice from the doctor—get a microwave.

Oh, to be a stay-at-home mother.

I have learned to be content whatever the circumstances.
(Philippians 4:11b)

Notice how I was ready to jump ship as soon as I bumped into hardship. It would be much better to say, "I've learned to be content whatever the circumstances." That would mean going through the situation well. (Following the doctor's advice helped.)

Going Downhill

Six twelve-year-old girls and I were scheduled to go downhill skiing on Saturday. I hadn't planned to go downhill skiing. I gave up that sport fifteen years ago when I spent more time getting back up on my skis than going down the hills. I would be going because I was a Girls' Club leader and six twelve-year-olds had very cunningly manipulated me.

I liked being a Girls' Club leader. These girls were impressionable and I wanted to give them all the good news I knew about Jesus. I wanted to do this by osmosis, but was stuck with the more difficult "lesson and example" method.

So why would I be taking them downhill skiing on Saturday?

It all began rather innocently at a regular club meeting. After a lesson on "Rejoicing Always," the girls and I were going through our badge books picking possible projects for the months to come. Babysitting, Bicycling, Camping—"Let's go camping!" came the enthusiastic cry.

"In the winter?" I questioned.

"We could go skiing," they said.

"Let's go to a ski resort for a weekend."

"Financially, out of the question," I said.

"We could raise the money," they offered.

"Uh...huh," I mused.

"We could have a bake sale," they offered.

"Do you know how much a weekend at a ski resort costs?" I asked.

"A hundred dollars," they figured. Then the planning began in earnest. Betty would phone the resorts for prices.

Everyone would bake for the sale. Deb would bring a money box. Patsy would fill a jar with jelly beans and Diane would bring a stuffed animal for the guessing games.

"Will you take us skiing if we get enough money?" they questioned hopefully.

"Sure," I good-naturedly agreed. It was like promising to eat all the cheese on the moon if they could get me there.

The rest of the meeting was spent writing on 35 slips of hand-torn paper: *Please bring money for our Bake Sale next week. Signed: The Discoverers*. There was a place for my initials as the approving leader.

I found the whole exercise rather promising as this was the first time all six girls were in total eager agreement on anything.

"If we don't make enough money we can always give it to charity," Cathy suggested.

"That's a good idea," I beamed.

"The Good Shepherd Centre, maybe," contributed Thelma.

We prayed the bake sale would go well.

The following week the girls all showed up with plastic containers filled with an assortment of cut-up squares, cakes, and cookies. There was even popcorn. The jelly beans and the stuffed animal were there too.

The bake sale went very well. We raised $26.80 selling to fellow club members and the ladies group which was meeting at the church that Friday evening.

Betty reported she couldn't phone ski resorts. "My parents won't let me call long-distance," she explained.

Then (and I don't quite know how this happened) the issue became whether to spend a day downhill skiing at a local winter sports park or cross-country skiing at the conservation area. Going on an overnight trip to a resort was never again mentioned and the idea of giving the money to a charity was completely snowed under. I tried uncovering it several times, but to no avail.

It was only a matter of time before they decided on downhill skiing. Never mind that the bake sale returns would barely cover lift charges. They could all get the money for ski equipment rentals from private resources, namely their parents.

There it was. I had said I would take them skiing if they could come up with the money. That was why I would be taking six twelve-year-olds downhill skiing Saturday. That was also why I was fighting a powerful urge to pray for rain.

Above all, love each other deeply, because love covers over a multitude of sins. (1 Peter 4:8)

Year later, as I contemplate my time spent with these girls, I realize I don't remember them as individuals. I had a whole year to establish relationships and I didn't do it. I focussed on the agenda: give these girls the good news about Jesus. At the time I didn't comprehend the full significance of Jesus in me (and in them). Instead of concentrating on being a Girls' Club leader who had a message and kept her word, I could have come to know each girl and cared about her, been interested in her life and her concerns. The osmosis would have been possible.

Shamed by the Dust

On Monday morning an unpleasant odour greeted us in the kitchen. It smelled slightly of rotten cabbage. Over breakfast Marty and I and all four children speculated its source. The odour seemed to be stronger when the refrigerator door was open.

Feeling slightly guilty I cautiously explored the interior of the refrigerator. In the half year since I began working part-time outside the home, I'd been overlooking certain housekeeping duties—I hadn't even thought about scouring my oven or thoroughly cleaning out my fridge.

"Ah-ha," I said, "it must be this half cabbage I've been ignoring for the past several weeks." I hurried the offending article to the trash container in the garage. It was good to have the problem solved before leaving for work.

But at 3:30 that afternoon when the kids and I stepped in the door the odour was unmistakable. Simply removing the supposed culprit had obviously not been enough.

A sniffing inspection told me everything inside the refrigerator was polluted.

I unplugged the monster and emptied it, washing every jar, bottle, dish and plastic container. I threw out bits of mouldy cheese and dried-out meat. I removed and washed the racks and trays. I scrubbed the inside walls until they shone. My nose told me the problem had been beat. I loaded the bottles, jars and plastic containers back in, and smugly, started up the appliance.

I even had a half hour left to get supper ready before Marty was due home.

23

It wasn't five minutes before I realized the odour had returned. Once more I pulled the refrigerator plug. The odour diminished. "It must be a mechanical problem," I surmised.

I knew whom to call. An excellent Christian appliance repairman who operated a business from his home just three blocks away had been recommended to us. I'd been looking for an opportunity to try him out. As fellow Christians we might even discuss something more interesting than refrigerators.

"Let's see, he was the one with the "fish" in his ad in the yellow pages. Yes, there he was: H.S. Jenkins, fast reliable service."

H.S. showed up about an hour later as we were just finishing our fish sticks, french fries, peas and canned applesauce.

He started up the refrigerator. He sniffed. He wrinkled his nose. He moved the fridge away from the wall and sneezed and sneezed and sneezed.

"I guess I should clean back there," I mumbled.

"Most places are like this," he assured me between sneezes. "I'm just allergic to dust." He opened the refrigerator door. I beamed as the interior gleamed out at him. He stopped sneezing.

I thought he might comment on the spotless condition of my refrigerator, but he asked, "Has milk or anything spilled in here lately?"

"No," I answered, slightly annoyed.

"Yes," Marty contradicted. "Saturday morning when I got up—you were still in bed—"(he gave me a meaningful look) "I found a puddle of milk on the floor in front of the fridge. There was a hole in one of the bags you bought Friday night." (I got another meaningful look.)

H.S. had the answer then. He ripped open the bottom of the fridge and pulled out masses of soggy, smelly insulation.

"Here's your problem. The milk seeped in down here." He stood up. "You might as well do this yourself," he said, wrinkling his nose. "Take all this garbage out. Dry up the area.

Sprinkle in some baking soda and replace the insulation. I had another client with the very same problem."

He left, a few dollars richer. Marty and I got busy following his instructions and, of course, I also cleaned behind the refrigerator.

Filth is so embarrassing.

> *Who may ascend the hill of the Lord? Who may stand in his holy place? He who has clean hands and a pure heart... (Psalm 24:3–4a)*

The psalmist is concerned with ascending the hill of the Lord and standing in His holy place—noble desires requiring clean hands and a pure heart. At this point in my life I was not thinking about ascending the hill of the Lord or standing in His holy place. Those destinations weren't on my earthly radar screen. Besides, my hands were dirty and my heart impure. *They smelled slightly of rotten cabbage.* And I didn't recognize the source of the odour. I needed the Holy Spirit's help.

Alone at the Helm

School concerts are okay when I know most of the kids and when my children are on stage at least half the time; but when a school program becomes a Fine Arts Festival with the most talented senior children from seven area schools participating, and my kid is only one small voice in an elaborate choir, I send Marty. I'd rather be at home reading a book, any book.

On the evening of this particular Fine Arts Festival with the most talented senior students from seven area schools participating, Marty had a meeting. I thought of not going to the festival, but Angela was in the choir. She had practised for months.

As I hesitated, Allison, 8, Paul, 6, and Michelle, 3, jumped up and down, eager to go. They convinced me it would be fun.

Adhering to instructions drilled into Angela by the choir director, we arrived at the auditorium a half hour before curtain time. I let Paul and Allison choose our seats. They chose the balcony, top back row, very near the ceiling. Michelle clung to me afraid she would tumble down 20 metres to the stage.

When the program finally began, Michelle was a little less frightened. She was also ready to go home. To draw her into the festival, I pointed out Angela in the choir on stage proudly singing, "All Night, All Day."

Michelle watched intently, but when the number was over she grabbed my face in her little hands and whispered loudly, "I want to go home."

I wondered why I hadn't brought her special *blanky*.

Each of the seven schools performed at least two numbers, and the audience participated six times. After each number Michelle grabbed my face and whispered, "I want to go home, now." According to my calculations, Michelle grabbed my face 21 times.

The last item on the program was an announcement that refreshments were available in the cafeteria. This stirred Paul, who had been sweetly sitting, eyes fixed on the stage for nearly two hours.

"Refreshments!" he said.

"We'll have something at home," I decided as we slowly filed out.

Paul didn't like the decision. He tugged at my purse and whined, "I'm hungry."

Michelle made it a chorus, "I can't walk."

As I bent to lift her, I lost track of Allison, who drifted obliviously along with the crowd—the part heading toward the cafeteria. Angela appeared and asked if we are going for refreshments.

"No, it's late. We'll get something at home," I repeated. This set Paul to renewed whining and purse pulling. I sent Angela after Allison with instructions to meet us at the door.

Finally—it seemed hours later—we were trotting among large gently falling snowflakes across the parking lot toward our station wagon.

The snow had a refreshing effect. Paul began to run. His dress shoes did him in. He was flat on his behind and wailing. Allison kindly helped him to his feet, but the wailing continued.

I walked faster. The wailing stopped. I slowed down, and took Paul's hand as we continued our trek. Michelle sat heavily on one of my arms while Paul dragged the other.

"I'm sitting in the front," pouted Paul.

"Okay," I answered. I assumed he wanted the much coveted spot by the window.

"I sit side you, mommy?" Michelle questioned.

"Yes, sweetheart," I agreed.

When I opened the car door, Paul who I had been pulling along like a stone weight, was strapped, as if by magic, neatly into the front centre seat belt. Wearily I set Michelle on the driver's seat.

"Paul, could you move over? You know Michelle asked to sit there."

He refused. Michelle whimpered.

I pulled the car brush out, slammed the door, and slowly brushed the car windows, praying for help.

When I opened the car door again, Paul hadn't moved and Michelle was still whimpering. Angela and Allison sat patiently in the back seat. I told them I would be out playing in the snow until they fixed the problem.

I brushed the hood and the headlights. I peered through the window. I brushed the roof. My feet were soaked. I peered in again. Paul had finally moved over one seat. Michelle had been strapped in front and centre. I got behind the wheel. Paul screamed and cried and generally carried on.

I looked at him and told him he was ruining the whole evening for everyone. "And, you are not getting a snack at home either. You are going right to bed."

"I'm going to run away."

"Good bye!" I said coldly.

He didn't leave; instead he used his secret weapon.

"I won't kiss you ever again. I don't love you."

"Too bad...I love you anyway; but I will probably get a babysitter for you next time we go anywhere; and if you don't stop carrying on I'll think of more rotten things."

By this time I was absently steering our way out of the parking lot with 500 other cars.

The mood on the short drive home was subdued.

"How was it?" Marty greeted us at the door.

I glared at him, "Next time, you go."

I don't ever, ever want to be a single parent.

> *All a man's ways seem right to him, but the Lord weighs the heart. (Proverbs 21:2)*

As I examine my cold-hearted, selfish, self-centred mothering, I can only ask God to forgive me. At the time I thought I was totally justified and even wise. It's not whether I should have taken the kids for refreshments, or let Paul sit where he wanted. I may have done some right things, but my attitude was very wrong. God looks at the heart.

Be Careful What You Pray

If you believe, you will receive whatever you ask for in prayer. (Matthew 21:22)

Our family of six was having a wonderful time until the day, a week and a half into our two-week camping vacation, when I made a simple request of the Lord, which He answered almost immediately. For a week and a half the weather had been warm, but not muggy; the beaches were inviting, yet not crowded; the campsites were roomy and private; and the friends we chose to camp with were very companionable.

That's why I prayed the prayer; things were so ideal I wanted the vacation to go on forever. I couldn't bear the thought of going home to the hot dirty city, 100 kilometres from the nearest clean beach. I knew the vacation couldn't go on forever, so I prayed, "Lord, help us to be happy to go home to Hamilton." If I had thought about it, I might have kept the prayer unspoken at least until the final day of our vacation.

The very afternoon of the day of my prayer, we were merrily biking back to our campsite after a refreshing swim when, too late, we realized something peculiar had happened to the camp roads.

"Why is the road wet? It hasn't rained," I wondered as I pedalled to keep up with the rest of the family.

Then it dawned on me, "They must have sprayed to keep the dust down." But the water didn't seem to be soaking in or running off. It simply sat on the road congealing with the oily dust into dirty little globules.

Wet globules were clinking up inside my fenders. At least I had fenders; Paul had the goo flinging up his back.

We reached our campsite, looking like mud-derby participants. For the next hour we cleaned ourselves, and for the next two days we couldn't go to or from the tap, the washrooms, the playground or the beach without bringing along cakes of mud.

By the time the traffic had packed the muck into a hard surface, I was fervently looking forward to city sidewalks.

Also we were being plagued by park wildlife. Mosquitoes arrived in swarms which meant we were using sticky mosquito spray. A person covered with a layer of mosquito spray, crawling into a sleeping bag, is guaranteed to long for a warm bath and clean linens.

Raccoons were becoming bold and pesky. At nightfall they gathered among the trees just beyond the light of our campfire, sometimes not even waiting for us to retire before combing the site for crumbs and scraps. But coons weren't the worst of the scavengers.

On the second to final night of our vacation, when Marty got up to put out the inadequately doused, flaring campfire, he came nose-to-nose with a skunk. He dove back into the tent; all threat of the fire banished from his thoughts. A skunk does worry a person—especially after a prayer like the one I prayed. Strange, the park literature didn't mention skunks.

By Saturday, our final day, I was more than happy to go home; yet I was somewhat at odds about thanking the Lord for answering my prayer.

Trust in the Lord with all your heart and lean not on your own understanding... (Proverbs 3:5)

I believe God answered my request to be happy to go home to the city, to teach me about prayer. He showed me a "yes" to my every whim and desire could put this world in big trouble. I'm certainly not capable of seeing the whole picture— I don't even play chess very well. On the other hand, when I pray accurately, according to the good and perfect will of the Lord, He can get a lot done by answering my prayers. If all Christians prayed His good and perfect will, His kingdom would be here.

Bird Watching

When I meet or read about people with hobbies that involve collecting or knowing all about a subject, I become jealous. "I would love to do that," I thought impulsively as I scanned a colourful eight-volume stamp collection. As I read about a double-headed 1812 penny, it occurred to me, "Coin collecting would be a pleasant escape."

Then I saw a newspaper picture of an elderly lady smiling lovingly across a room full of 4302 bells, not one of them the same, and I thought I could start a similar collection. If I wrote to her she might give me some of her traders.

Nothing substantial ever developed from my impulsive thoughts, but I went on with the bright hope that someday one of these hobbies might become a passion for me.

That was my simple desire when I signed up for a bird walk early on a Saturday morning. "All a person needs for this hobby," I thought, "is a good bird book and a set of binoculars." I borrowed the binoculars and planned to invest in a *Peterson Field Guide*. As the morning progressed, I realized there was more to this hobby than meets the eye. It's also a matter of listening. You should be able to distinguish one bird's twirps and chirps from another. There are tapes available to help you learn them, I was told. If you get good—which serious birders strive to do—you will be able to imitate bird calls and the birds will come out of the woods to look at you; for as it was explained to us, "Birds have an inborn sense of curiosity, one which overpowers their fear of many things."

"Look, there is a pileated woodpecker."

"Where?"

"There, to the left behind the dead tree at 11 o'clock."

That's nicely said, but how do I, who don't know left from right, get my binoculars to the correct spot? No matter which way I point them, all I get is a blur of leaves.

I was still vainly searching for the pileated woodpecker, when in rapid succession the guide pointed out a wigeon, a grebe and a tern on the lake to our right; and an avid bird watcher in the group called our attention to a yellow-bellied something-or-other.

The guide helpfully told us how to distinguish these birds by their markings and the shape of their beaks. My interest was caught by a woman carrying powerful, compact binoculars and wearing a jaunty, birder's hat. I could tell she was enjoying herself immensely. On the way back to our starting point, I struck up a conversation.

"You seem to know a lot about birds."

"Not as much as I would like. I've only been doing it three years. I love it. It's a compulsion. I carry my binoculars everywhere. I plan my holidays along bird migration routes. Oh, look, there's a northern waterthrush. I pull the car over on the way to work if I catch a glance of an unusual tail pattern or rump patch."

Later a truth dawned on me: God made a great variety of birds and an even greater variety of people. Some of us are just not cut out to be bird watchers.

Blessed are they who keep his statutes and seek him with all their heart. (Psalm 119:2)

God created and loves each one of us, whether we are yellow-bellied, have an unusual rump patch or act like a woodpecker. And, just as He blesses birds with "an inborn sense of curiosity," God puts inside each one of us a longing and a desire to be part of something bigger than ourselves. That longing ultimately draws us toward Him.

Gift from Dad

"Dad's giving us some manure for our garden since we're leaving the kids here with them and we'll have room in the car," Marty quietly informed me while we were comfortably sitting on the couch in his parents' living room.

"No!" I said. "We don't need manure. You're not putting that stuff in the back of our station wagon. Manure stinks!"

Marty was caught in the middle. He knew where I stood and he had to live with me, but he didn't want to hurt his father's feelings. Now that Marty's dad was retired he had lots of time to think about the many ways he could help his children.

Up to that point, he had given us regular, mostly appreciated stuff: a jar of jam, a hunk of cheese, stalks of rhubarb, part of a pig, half a cow, letters of advice; but at manure I had to draw the line.

It must have been the way I phrased the question that turned things against me: "What are you going to do about this, Marty?"

"I'm going to take Dad's offer. He's got it all ready for us. He really wants us to have it."

When Marty gave Dad the go ahead, Dad practically flew out of the house and was back in mere minutes with a wheelbarrow piled up with not one, not two, but six bags—big, green plastic garbage bags full—of manure: three chicken and three cow.

As Marty and his dad piled the stuff into the back of our compact station wagon, one bag developed a hole. Kindly, Dad didn't load that one.

That left five bags piled high in the back, three chicken manure and two cow dung; "dry stuff" I was assured.

I actually stopped thinking about it until about an hour later when it was time to leave. Dad casually mentioned, "There might be a slight odour."

I gagged as I put myself in the car. It was a very hot day. Marty thanked his dad. Imagine that! Then his dad had the gall to ask me if I intended to thank him as well.

I glared at him, "This is the worst trick you ever played on us." He playfully stuck out his tongue in response.

Unfortunately we couldn't open the back window; it wasn't that kind of car. I rode along with my nostrils pulled in and my head out the side window. A few miles down the road, I noticed some green garbage bags piled beside the road. Marty saw them too. We looked at each other and he pulled over backing along to where the bags were, considering unloading our putrid cargo.

"What will we tell my dad?" he wondered. "No, I can't do it. Just stick your head further out the window."

Some miles later he apologized, "If I had known it would be this bad, I wouldn't have taken this load."

Every time we came to a red light I leaned a little further out. For the first time in my life I envied the giraffe. Fortunately most of the trip was expressway. Unfortunately some of it was through a major city with lots of holiday traffic.

Finally two-and-a-half hours later we were home. Marty unloaded. Marty washed and scrubbed the carpeted trunk area. Marty could not get rid of the ammonia smell.

When Marty's parents came at the end of the week to return the children, my annoyance was at simmer. It usually only bubbled into resentment and anger when I got into the ammonia-reeking car. But when Marty's dad innocently inquired about the trip home, I exploded.

This time Marty backed me up, "Yes, Dad, it stunk."

"I can't understand. It was dry manure—except that bit of wet rained-on stuff on top. Yes, that must have done it. Got a reaction going. I didn't think it would do that."

"You know, Dad," I said as my anger dissipated, "This will make a good story."

Marty's dad saw the possibility but wanted me to change the main character to a well-meaning uncle. Marty didn't think so, neither did his mom, nor did I.

> *Get rid of all bitterness, rage and anger, brawling and slander, along with every form of malice. Be kind and compassionate to one another, forgiving each other, just as in Christ God forgave you. (Ephesians 4:31–32)*

An attitude of unforgiveness festers into bitterness and like the manure in our vehicle taints everything with its rank odour long after the original situation is cleaned up. It was important for me to clear the air by forgiving my father-in-law. I acknowledge it was easier to forgive him because he admitted he was wrong, and because I had a story. Regrettably, although I chose to forgive Dad, I certainly wasn't ready to be kind and compassionate.

We All Have Different Talents

In a family with children, birthdays cakes must be provided as the occasion demands. In our family, buying a ready-made cake has always been considered cheating. But I dislike baking. It is messy and time-consuming and the better the product, the sooner I have to bake again. Fortunately Angela, the eleven-year-old in our family, sees baking differently. She thrives on it. She searches cookbooks and contrives concoctions I would never dream of attempting.

For a full year after Angela discovered her pleasure, I didn't bake as much as a cookie. Angela took care of all the family baking needs. It was wonderful. Then at a most inconsiderate time, two days before her sister Allison's ninth birthday party to which seven little friends had been invited, Angela broke her ankle.

I had to admit it would be almost cruel to expect her to gather and measure ingredients while hopping about on crutches with a swollen, splinted, throbbing ankle.

I was back in the kitchen, measuring cup in hand. I cheated somewhat: I bought a mix, and ready-made icing on sale for $1.49. I prepared the mix and poured it into two round pans without mishap. Some minutes after the cake had baked, I flipped each pan onto a plate. Half of each cake layer flopped down onto its plate. The other half stuck to the bottom of the tin. Having anticipated some such crisis, I calmly found a spatula to pry out the rest of the cake and let each piece drop carefully onto its other part.

The icing was rather stiff in its canister so I diluted it with a few splats of milk. When it had the "desired consistency," I spread this onto one overturned cake layer. It took great skill and lightness of touch. A heavy hand would have reduced the cake to a mass of crumbs.

Very deftly I flipped the second layer over the first, by halves as one half stuck onto the plate.

I generously iced all around the double layers in a swirling crumb-filled pattern. This done there was no icing left to cover the top of the cake. Would five nine-year-olds notice? Of course they would: nine-year-olds can be very critical. I carefully robbed the swirls on the sides of the cake, only gouging the cake once. I would have to remember to turn that side away from Allison and her guests.

After what seemed an eternity, the whole cake was covered.

For the finishing touches, I whipped up some decorator icing with confectionery sugar and water. What I took for the correct consistency was a little runny, but I didn't figure that out until it was on the cake.

In a generous mood I scrawled *Happy* across the cake. Very nice, correct spelling, and no room left for *Birthday*. Oh well, I could tuck *Day* down at the bottom. Then I made nine little blobs which were supposed to look like flowers, but they came out blobs in a random pattern.

As an afterthought I planted nine raspberry candies on the blobs. Quickly before any more afterthoughts might occur I hid the whole thing under a cake cover.

When my best friend walked in several minutes later I pulled up the cover, mumbling, "It's a bit of a disaster. I hope Allison's friends aren't too critical."

"It looks like a mother's love," she comforted. This is why she is my best friend.

She was right. Nobody said anything about the cake; they were wondering why the pizza was burnt. Allison kindly explained it to them, "My mom is getting to be a worse and worse cook."

Am I blooming yet? My life seems more like blobs in random pattern.

But God was with him and rescued him from all his troubles. He gave Joseph wisdom and enabled him to gain the goodwill of Pharaoh king of Egypt; so he made him ruler over Egypt and all his palace. (Acts 7:9b–10)

I'm sure while in jail Joseph didn't revel in his predicament, but with the Lord's direction he did make the best of each crumby circumstance and ultimately became the ruler of Egypt, rescuing the land and his own family from starvation. Our lives might seem like blobs with no pattern, but we can trust the Lord to line things up, just as our family trusted Angela's ankle would heal. Our role is to go through each situation well, with love.

Food for Thought

If I were given a loaf of store-bought white bread, or by accident happened to mistakenly pick up a white loaf instead of the 100 per cent whole wheat our family customarily eats, I would likely leave it in the bread box to dry out or mould.

To my way of thinking white bread is useless nutritionally (except for the few vitamins with which it is artificially enriched). We may as well eat a bowl of sawdust as a slice of white bread. In fact, I might even throw out a loaf of white bread *before* it goes mouldy.

In the past, I never associated worthless white bread with the bread at the Lord's Supper. I never gave the actual cube of bread at the Lord's Supper serious thought: I usually tried to think of Jesus dying on the cross for me—unworthy, blessed me. The tastelessness and texture of the little white square was incidental. I'll admit the swallow of wine awakened a warm pleasantness as I contemplated the love of my Saviour, but the bread was just there to be chewed.

This changed, when my husband, the newly elected elder, requested, "Dear, could you buy four square loaves of white Wonder Bread when you go shopping this week?"

I was aghast, "You know we don't eat white bread."

"It's for Lord's Supper on Sunday."

Oh, that was different. On Thursday morning, I found myself in the grocery store carefully choosing four, square white loaves of Wonder Bread. I tossed my wholesome whole wheat into the grocery cart as usual, but the white bread I stacked gently on top of my three bags of milk.

At the cash register I ever so carefully placed the white bread away from the other groceries so it would not be squeezed. I even bagged it and carried it out to the car myself, while the carry-out person brought the rest of the stuff in the cart.

At home I immediately arranged the white loaves in my freezer. My freezer generally looks like a bargain basement table, with a tumble of meat and various garden vegetables, but I was able to tidy up a corner for this bread. Marty wanted it frozen so it would be easier to cut.

On Saturday evening he got out the cutting board and the large knife. In twenty minutes he had the crusts removed and all four loaves cubed and re-bagged. Then he groaned and ran out to the 24-hour Miracle Mart for another loaf; he had forgotten to leave a few strips for the minister to break.

Sunday morning Marty left for church extra early to help prepare the communion table. He would be serving as well.

In church when the bread was passed, my piece had a touch of brown crust on it. "I'll have to mention it to Marty," I thought. After all, Jesus body should only be represented by pure white bread.

"This is the body of Christ. Remember and believe," instructed the minister.

That evening I stayed home with our younger children, while Marty, Angela and Allison went to church again. The girls walked home popping leftover bread cubes into their mouths. (They understood the actual Lord's Supper was for grown-ups. Marty and I had explained to them, that although they have accepted Jesus into their hearts, this wouldn't be acknowledged by our church until they were old enough to help run the place.)

"These are good!" Angela exclaimed. "May we take some to school for snack, tomorrow?"

I wouldn't let them: an oatmeal cookie would be more nourishing, and children happily munching on a pile of Lord's Supper bread cubes at the Christian school might appear disrespectful.

For anyone who eats and drinks without recognizing the body of the Lord eats and drinks judgment on himself. That is why many among you are weak and sick, and a number of you have fallen asleep. (1 Corinthians 11:29–30)

The Lord's Supper has been given to us as a powerful reminder of Jesus' victory over sin, sickness and death. When I begin to see beyond ritual into that reality, the bread will truly become "Wonder" bread.

The Gift That Wasn't

The phone rang. It was Marnie. "Marian, I'm embarrassed to tell you this; I bought you a present."
"For me? You did?"
"For your family."
"What's the occasion?"
"Oh, just because you're nice and Marty and Allison had a birthday."
"So why are you embarrassed?"
"Well, because the present is so nice."
"That's embarrassing?"
"Yes, because I'm keeping it. I bought it for you on Friday, fell in love with it over the weekend, and I can't bear to part with it."
"Thanks, I guess." Marnie and I, good friends since high school, over 20 years ago, don't often buy each other presents, so I was sort of grateful for the thought. "What in the world is it?"
"It's a bird."
"You bought us a bird. Oh, Marnie thank you." Now I really was grateful. How many friends do you have who would buy you a bird and keep it for you?
You see, our four children had been bothering Marty and me for a pet and again this year we had promised to look into it. The truth is I don't like pets. I don't mind admiring someone else's pets, but I don't like to take care of a pet. If a pet came to me toilet-trained (that's flush toilet), I might reconsider.
It isn't that we haven't tried to meet our children's desire for animal friends. We took them to the zoo once and we've

lived next to people with rabbits and dogs. We've even owned goldfish, but they died. Our gerbils died too. So did the puppy we had for three days: the one that slept under the car.

"I knew you were looking for a pet and as soon as I saw her I thought of you," continued Marnie. "She's got a big cage and she talks."

"She talks?"

"It's a parrot."

"A parrot? You bought us a parrot? Expensive, I bet."

"Yeah, but that's okay. You're worth it."

That evening I told Marty and the kids, "Aunt Marnie bought us a pet."

"She did? What is it?" the kids chorused.

"It's a bird, a parrot, but we're not getting it because she fell in love with it."

"Aww." The disappointment was showing.

"But," I added, "we can go look at it and maybe think about getting one like it." Notice how I didn't commit myself.

Several evenings later we were introduced to Zack. (She was named before they figured out her sex.) She was a pretty green bird with a yellow patch on her head, orange eyes and several red and blue tail feathers.

"Hello," she said. "Tickle, tickle. Want a peanut? Thank you. Bye." She whistled, she barked and she meowed. The kids loved her.

"There's probably not another bird like her," Marnie said. "Nobody is allowed to say bad words in front of her: she learns words so fast."

I actually liked the bird. I liked her all the more because Marnie wasn't about to part with her, although she did promise we could baby-sit Zack sometime, maybe even for a few weeks when she moulted, because all those feathers would make Marnie's family sneeze.

Our children came home raving about Zack. Angela took to reading the want ads every evening. She only came across one parrot, but by the time we phoned it was gone.

Maybe I could talk the kids into settling for a bird-feeding station in the backyard.

"Which of you, if his son asks for bread, will give him a stone?" (Matthew 7:9)

My sentiment toward pets mirrored my attitude toward the Holy Spirit. It was okay for my sister-in-law to speak in tongues, but I was not interested in receiving that "gift" as she called it. Prophetic words, miracles, signs and wonders were all evidences of the Holy Spirit which I enjoyed reading about in the Bible, but I was not expecting to experience those things personally. Little did I know that in the not too distant future, even as Zack would come to live at our house, the Holy Spirit would captivate me.

A 40-Day Experience

It was exactly 40 days from the afternoon the doctor first said, "You could be going any time now," to the night our fifth child, Amanda, was finally born. I'm sure the doctor wouldn't have been so loose with his prediction if he had been the one continually preparing my household for the big birth day.

My very capable mother-in-law would be coming to take over on the home front while I was in the hospital, and to my mind it was essential that she know her son had a reasonably capable wife. This meant I had to make sure the laundry was caught up, the house tidy, clean sheets on all the beds, and enough food around for 21 meals.

To achieve these things is not so difficult, but to waddle through them every day for 40 days is a bit taxing especially at the any-minute stage in a pregnancy, when even putting on socks is a major physical feat.

What to do with our four other children at a moment's notice provided further complications. The basic plan was to send them next door until Marty's mother actually arrived. Jill, my wonderful next-door-neighbour, gave me her day-by-day schedule including family outings, shopping trips and overnight company. That way I could adjust immediate plans accordingly. On any given day she would advise me, "Don't have the baby between one and four this afternoon." Or, "Today is good; I'll be home except between seven and nine this evening."

False labour pains further complicated my life. You would think after giving birth four times previously, I would recognize genuine labour.

Haahh! I actually checked into the hospital twice with nothing tangible to show for my genuine effort not to have a home (or car) birth. It's embarrassing coming home from a three-hour hospital stay, still pregnant, never mind doing it twice.

At that stage I received much friendly advice: drink raspberry tea; wash and wax the floor; eat Chinese food; eat pizza; take castor oil; and the wisest of all, the baby will come when it's ready.

It occurred to me the Lord knew when that would be, but I sure wished He would let me in on the plan. I was beginning to doubt I was even pregnant.

Of course I was pregnant and Amanda was finally born "well cooked" as the doctor described her.

Full of the joy and wonder a new baby brings, I didn't give my forty days and forty nights of waiting another thought—until one summer day. As I pushed four-month-old Amanda down the sidewalk in her buggy, a lady behind a huge stomach waddled toward me. She moved ever so slowly, her feet pointing out duck fashion; but she had a blissful "soon I'll have something to show for this" look on her face.

"Thirty-nine weeks," she said when I asked how far along she was.

"Yes," I recalled, "I was 39 weeks for 40 days"—about the time it took me to realize the Lord was in charge.

> *"Now learn this lesson from the fig tree: As soon as its twigs get tender and its leaves come out, you know that summer is near. Even so, when you see all these things, you know that it is near, right at the door." (Matthew 24:32–33)*

Biblically, 40 is a number of trial and testing. It is a period of preparation. My 40 days involved constantly being ready for the big day. Several times I visited the hospital prematurely in anticipation of the event. Then even though I had tangible proof of my pregnancy, I began to doubt birth was imminent. Yes, Amanda was born and, yes, Jesus is coming back soon. We have to be ready constantly.

The 'Old' Dutch Mother

When I was in the hospital after giving birth to our first child, Angela, I shared the room with two other young, new mothers and an "old" Dutch woman. She must have been almost 40. She had four children at home. She missed them dearly and chatted with them on her bedside phone at least once a day.

We had a good time in that ward, the four of us. We talked and laughed, trading stories about our husbands.

Then on about day three, while the rest of us were still wincing over our stitches, Mrs. VanderZee, the "old" lady among us hopped out of bed and packed her things. The doctor had given her permission to return home to her family. She was eager to see her children for in those days and in that hospital children were not allowed to visit.

Before she left we all traded addresses and promised to keep in touch. We never told Mrs. VanderZee, but we three young mothers felt she was rather an anomaly and wondered how in the world having a fifth baby at her age could make her so happy. And her delight in going home to a house full of children with her tiny, completely dependant newborn was incomprehensible to us. Where would she get the energy?

The three of us took comfort in knowing at least when we returned to our quiet little abodes we would be able to sleep and rest while our babies slept.

In those first years we three young mothers kept in touch by phone and through visits. We even had joint birthday parties for our babies. There at the parties, we would wonderingly remember Mrs. VanderZee with whom we all exchanged Christmas cards. She couldn't get to the parties because she lived way out in the country and had five children.

Well, twelve years later, there I was (almost 40) in the hospital overjoyed with my fifth baby.

I missed my four other children dearly and talked to them on my bedside phone at least once a day. Their visit was the highlight of my stay in the hospital. They were all so very happy and excited about their new little sister.

One day a smiling young nurse who gave needles with a grin came to my bedside, a clipboard full of questions in her hand. She asked me how old I was. "Thirty-eight," I said.

She asked me how many children I had at home. "Four," I said.

"You must be Dutch," she concluded.

"What makes you think that?" (Why was I thinking of Mrs. VanderZee?)

"Well," she said, "Dutch people just seem to have lots of babies, regardless."

"Maybe they love each other," I conjectured.

"Maybe they don't know when to stop," she answered.

I know she found it incomprehensible that I could be truly delighted with my new baby, at my age. Actually now that I think about it, Mrs. VanderZee wasn't "old" at all!

> *This is love: not that we loved God, but that he loved us and sent his Son as an atoning sacrifice for our sins. (1 John 4:10)*

Just as I failed to grasp Mrs. VanderZee's overflowing love for her children until I had a family of my own, the unconditional love God has for His family is somewhat more understandable now that I have children. We are His children. He loves us simply for that reason.

A Greasy Situation

I don't remember exactly when the toilet stopped flushing properly, but it happened after several months of my recklessly throwing cooking grease and leftover gravy into the thing.

I had an inkling this was not an excellent way to dispose of grease, yet to my way of thinking it was better than pouring the stuff down the sink and not as messy as throwing it in the garbage. Suffice it to say, when the toilet drain began acting sluggish I felt responsible and poured further grease under a bush in the backyard.

In the meantime three minutes with a toilet plunger would unclog the toilet, but only temporarily. Bottles of *Liquid Plumber*, solutions of lye, and canisters of *Drano* (not to be used in toilet bowls) followed one another to the sewer. Nothing helped for long. I sent my husband Marty to the *Rent-All* for an auger. He "augered" for 20 minutes, with only a scratched toilet bowl to show for his efforts.

The toilet was becoming an embarrassment. As a family we instinctively began using the upstairs "john" only, but we never quite remembered to warn unwary guests about our faulty facilities until it was too late.

Then one Monday morning after a Sunday guest had suffered the indignity of using our washroom, I took dramatic action: I called a plumber. This was a last resort and something I did not do easily. In my experience plumbers had a way of pointing a person to her own stupidity and they generally charged a lot of money to do this.

"Has a kid dropped a toy in here?" he questioned.

"I was throwing grease down there for a while." I winced as I said it, but thought I might as well confess, as plumbers are able to figure out these things.

"Tut, tut, I won't slap your hand," he comforted. He plungered; he augered; he turned the water off; he removed the whole toilet; then he reached down into the hole in the floor and pulled out the culprit.

"There was something in the grease!" he announced triumphantly as he held up every dog's treasure, a thick five-inch soup bone.

I blushed and stammered and felt very foolish.

"These things happen," he said, kindly brushing aside my guilty feelings. Then he put everything back except the bone and scrawled out a bill for $65.

I thanked him as he left. I was relieved to have the problem solved.

Now, how was I going to face the family? I buried the bone in the garbage—a show-and-tell was not what I wanted.

That evening I announced to Marty and the kids, "The toilet is fixed." Of course they wanted to know details, which I reluctantly told them, playing down the size of the bone and the size of the bill. Being family, they understood. It's been two months now, and they hardly even mention it anymore!

> Then the man and his wife heard the sound of the Lord God as he was walking in the garden in the cool of the day, and they hid from the Lord God among the trees of the garden. (Genesis 3:8)

Why is it so difficult to take responsibility for doing something wrong? Why the shame? Ever since the Garden of Eden we've been prone to cover up and hide or even deny our mistakes. We do this big time when it comes to sin—even though Christ died on the cross to pay for every one of our sins. Our part is to be truthful; to confess our sins and turn from them as soon as we recognize them.

Sin and Anger

It was Thursday, 3:30 p.m. From my sickbed I heard the school kids jubilantly parade into the house. Listening to them, I surmised they each had a case of chocolate bars—those big almond bars that go for two dollars each.

I had been warned. An ominous letter about student funds and school trips had appeared several weeks ago. There was an escape clause in the letter. It mentioned that if you didn't wish to participate, you could feel free (or was it obliged?) to contribute in another way. Congenial person that I am, I usually endure these fund-raisers with a groan and a grin. I am also usually healthy and a fairly able trouble-shooter, but I had been bedridden with bronchitis for more than a week. That day I was just too sick to think much about three children (two of them under the age of twelve) each armed with $24 worth of chocolate.

The medicine the doctor had given me didn't seem to work. I was developing an itchy rash and I couldn't keep food down. My life was too miserable to think about chocolate. Under ordinary circumstances bells would have been going off in my head. I would have been disarming the children at the door with a kiss and a list of chocolate-selling campaign rules. That day I didn't sense danger, not even when I found out Friday was a professional activity day (that meant no school).

Friday morning before he left for work Marty instructed the children to be very good—which they were as they munched on chocolate bars in their rooms.

I didn't even recognize: "Here's two more dollars!", "Did you buy another one?", and "munch, munch" as warning signals. My trouble-shooting ability had abandoned me completely.

By Friday evening I was sick of being sick. Even though I was still feverish, nauseous, itchy and achy, the supper-making noises downstairs had me feeling left-out. I longed to be part of the functioning household again. Maybe I would just get out of bed and make an appearance. As I shuffled along the upstairs hall something oozed onto the soles of my warm bare feet. I checked under my left foot—it was chocolate, little bits of brown chocolate.

I got down on my hands and knees. The floor was covered with chocolate crumbs. I attempted to pick them up, but there were too many.

I checked the kids' rooms. The floors and the dressers were sprinkled with chocolate bits and discarded wrappers. In one room the quilt on the bed was smeared with chocolate. That did it. I picked up the quilt. I marched downstairs, dropped the quilt in the middle of the kitchen floor and screamed, "There's chocolate everywhere!" The happy supper-time chatter stopped as ten eyes stared at me and five mouths fell open.

I marched back upstairs, picked up several empty wrappers and marched back down. I threw them on the kitchen floor.

I marched back up once more, picked up the half empty boxes of bars with the money hanging out of the envelopes. I brought them into the kitchen and narrowly avoided slamming them into a thousand crumbs as I hoarsely screamed out against chocolate bar fund-raisers, "It's a fine way to raise money. Selling chocolate to yourselves!"

I yanked out the vacuum cleaner. By then the children were in tears. Marty looked at me and cautioned, "You'll kill yourself." I ignored him and marched back upstairs with the vacuum to suck up the offending chocolate crumbs. By the time I finished vacuuming, my anger was spent.

"*In your anger do not sin.*" (Ephesians 4:26a)

Did I sin?

The Prodigal

Angela wanted a dog. She never passed up an opportunity to say so. I didn't want a pet of any sort and adamantly said, "No." Of course Angela's younger sisters and brother were on her side.

Secretly my husband was too; but Marty knew how much I didn't want one, so he quietly watched the campaign progress.

I didn't want to feed or walk a mutt and I absolutely didn't want to clean up after one. Angela begged and bargained. She would feed the dog, walk the dog and even scoop the dog. I didn't believe her.

She argued; I argued back. She tempted me with a glorious promise. She said she would keep her room tidy to show she was responsible enough to take care of a dog. I laughed for she was promising the impossible. She smiled for she knew she had found the path to her pet.

She immediately straightened her room. She organized her dresser. She hung her clothes in the closet. She put her books on the shelf. And best of all, she quit stowing candy wrappers, pencils, hair barrettes and dirty laundry under her bed.

I was impressed. Angela didn't miss the opportunity, "See I am responsible enough to have a dog."

"It won't last," I said. It didn't, but it took almost a month before I discovered clothes on her floor and candy wrappers under her bed.

Of course by then I was hooked on the neat room and effectively lost the pet battle by saying, "Your room doesn't look like a dog." Angela smiled and efficiently tidied up.

"Your room doesn't look like a dog," held magic. For me it meant an instantly tidy room. For Angela, of course, it meant she would get a dog eventually.

Reluctantly I found myself saying, "Maybe after our holidays."

At once a chewed-up dog house appeared. Grandpa came to re-trim and re-shingle this garage sale acquisition for us. Then Marty fenced in the yard. The reality of a dog was closing in on me.

I was still unpacking vacation gear when Marty and the kids rushed over to the Society for Prevention of Cruelty to Animals (SPCA), just to look, they said.

They came home with a dog. He was a young but full-grown collie-cross with short cinnamon hair. He acted friendly and wasn't a barker. I resigned myself to his presence.

The kids loved him. They showed him his backyard domain and his dog house, explaining that Mom didn't want him in the real house.

The very afternoon of the day we acquired our nameless pet, Marty and I had a local wedding to attend. Before we could go Marty felt compelled to vacuum the van. For some reason there were little brown and white dog hairs on all the seats. After the wedding ceremony it began to rain, so we slipped home. We were met by tearful children, "The dog is gone." They showed us a narrow gap in the fence. I managed to contain my inappropriate happiness.

The kids had already inundated the neighbourhood with lost-dog posters and recruited neighbourhood children to ride bicycles up and down the streets looking.

Where was that *rascal*?

Marty promised to scout around, but first he drove me to the wedding reception where I sat, unaccompanied, wondering about my sad family. Meanwhile, Marty cruised the streets in vain, in what had become a pouring rainstorm. He arrived at the reception just as the newlyweds were leaving.

"At least he has a dog tag," I comforted.

"That's still in my pocket," Marty admitted sheepishly.

We returned to our unhappy, pet-less abode. Marty phoned the SPCA. They remembered our wonderful animal and promised to return him to us if he were picked up.

Then the rain stopped, the sun came out, and a neighbour brought the news. He had caught a glimpse of Rascal (for that was his name now) up the street rubbing noses through a fence, with a girl dog.

That evening there was joy in our home. As for me, I identified with the elder brother in the parable of the prodigal son.

> *"The older brother became angry and refused to go in. So his father went out and pleaded with him."* (Luke 15:28)

The displeasure I felt in sharing my home with a dog and my animosity toward Rascal are reminiscent of the anger the older brother expressed at the love their father showed to his contrite brother. It is also very similar to the way we Christians sometimes feel and express ourselves when the lost and broken try to join our church families.

Life with a dog

Our household was complete: five kids and a dog. But all was not sunshine and roses. Rascal was making this homemaker extremely grumpy.

I suppose he was just living up to his name. We should have called him "Sleepy" or "Gentleman." I didn't hate him, exactly. He did have big loveable, brown eyes—much like my husband's,—and he was ever so friendly. He would knock you over asking for a pat on the head. If he had been someone else's pet I might have liked him just fine—I simply resented his changing the dynamics of our household.

I could overlook the few hundred dollars we spent on his fence, his needles, his neutering, his several types of dog food—he wouldn't eat our first two choices—and his leash which he broke within a week. And it's not that I had to feed Rascal or walk him or clean up after him. As she promised, Angela did that.

My role became to remind her to do these things. My conversation with Angela seemed to be limited to: "When are you going to walk the dog? .....feed the dog? .....clean up the crap?" This was not my idea of enlightening conversation. It bordered on nagging.

My main complaint was that Rascal took over the backyard. Little kids were afraid to play there. In pre-Rascal days five-year-old Michelle's little friends would visit every day. From the kitchen window I could watch them on the swing set, at the playhouse or in the sandbox.

Now I never saw Michelle or her friends. They were usually in someone else's backyard.

Instead I could watch Rascal chewing on sandbox toys, tearing my clothes off the line or digging holes in the grass. Or I might spend my time attempting to clean the deck which was always covered in muddy paw prints. Actually, there was no real need to clean the deck as we never sat there anymore. We sat on the front porch. It was just too difficult to enjoy a mug of coffee with Rascal nuzzling up.

I got into the habit of taking a vote at the dinner table: "Who wants to get rid of Rascal?" I usually did this after the dog had personally wronged one of his fans. In the beginning it was me versus the rest of the family, but slowly they began to see things my way.

Paul came on side after Rascal chewed up his favourite squirt gun.

Allison decided she'd had enough when she'd been reduced to tears one too many times. Allison saw it as her duty to visit with Rascal at least once a day, out of pure pity. Of course he loved her for it, knocked her down and licked her face. She couldn't take it anymore.

Marty wanted the dog gone after Rascal unwound the garden hose and began eating it.

Pretty soon everyone was with me, except Angela who had kept her room tidy for months just to get a pet, and baby Amanda who didn't vote.

Then one fine day, Angela admitted she was tired of being dragged around the neighbourhood chasing squirrels. She finally voted to end Rascal's stay with us.

I kissed her.

Rascal went back to the SPCA.

Now I hate to admit this, but I miss him. We all do. The way Angela sees it, "At least we still have baby Amanda."

> *Offer hospitality to one another without grumbling. (1 Peter 4:9)*

The dog was changing my household and I wasn't happy until he was gone. Similarly, the broken and needy who try to join our church fellowships often come up against those among us running a quiet, patient campaign to see them gone. We count up and point out their misdeeds and setbacks; we avoid them; we pity them and only allow ourselves to love them after they've left.

A Sunday Morning Alternative

As we sped along the expressway in the family van at 7:45 in the morning, my sluggish-passenger-self noticed a driver in the car beside us with a Tim Horton's coffee in her hand. I knew that was what I wanted, but it was Sunday and I would rather not be the reason someone had to work today.

Our family was planning to spend the day with friends two hours away in the country. We hoped to meet them at their ten o'clock church service.

Although it was drizzling, the forecast had promised Indian summer so we'd put on our light jackets in anticipation. About half an hour down the road my feet started feeling cold.

Outside the drizzle was striving to be a flurry. I mentioned my cold feet to Marty who turned up the heat. Several minutes later my feet still felt cold. In fact they were becoming colder.

"We'll have to have the heater checked," said Marty, somewhat annoyed, for he had recently had the van in for its annual fall tune-up.

As I sat uncomfortably cool, privately wishing for a coffee, the miles passed beneath us and the orange needle on the temperature gauge began to crawl up around to the top of normal, close to the dangerous red area. Marty wondered if he should be alarmed as we pulled up to an intersection in a small town just past halfway to our destination. He stopped wondering when steam rose around us from beneath the dashboard. We pulled over to the shoulder of the road, our heads enveloped in vapour.

"What now?" he questioned.

"Probably nothing is open on Sunday morning," I mentioned helpfully.

Allison voiced her concern, "You mean we'll be stuck here for the rest of our lives?"

Marty got out to check under the hood and discovered a hole in the heater hose. Somehow this knowledge reduced our catastrophe to a troublesome inconvenience.

We waited for the motor to cool; then we coasted over to a small plaza where we spied a phone booth. Marty pulled out his Motor League card, the one with the long distance numbers on it. He and I pooled our change to make the call. We came up with $1.80.

The operator told Marty to deposit $1.85. He ran back to the van to ask Michelle to raid the Sunday school money in her change purse. Unfortunately she had left it at home "by an accident," she said.

Marty tried to charge the call to our home number, but of course there was no one there to confirm that he belonged to that number.

"What shall I do?" Marty asked the operator in exasperation.

"Get a calling card," was the bright reply.

"On a Sunday morning?"

"That might be difficult," she agreed.

So, instead of calling the Motor League, Marty phoned our friends—collect. They accepted the charges and even promised to come to our rescue if we were still stranded after church.

Then we spotted a seven-day-a-week donut shop.

Marty went in to inquire about local service stations. Yes, there was one that would open in half an hour at ten. It was just down the hill.

When Marty returned to his shivering family in the crippled van he suggested we spend our time inside the warm, comfortable donut shop.

Eight-year-old Paul balked, "It's Sunday. We shouldn't make people work."

I pulled out the example of Jesus in the cornfield, "The Sabbath was made for man, not man for the Sabbath."

We trotted inside to order hot chocolate for the kids and I got my much desired coffee. We might have ordered donuts as well but there were only a few stale-looking muffins available.

We sat at two tables. The coffee was disappointingly mediocre. We watched an information show about a conservation area in Alberta, emitting from the television at the back of the shop.

When we left about an hour later we thanked the proprietor who had been sympathetic to our dilemma.

At the garage a personable young man replaced our hose. He charged $1 for the hose, $5 for the work and $10.50 for a can of anti-freeze. By 10:30 we were back on the road.

Paul summed up the whole morning with the words, "I learned one thing: I would rather be in church than do this other stuff."

For I desire mercy, not sacrifice, and acknowledgment of God rather than burnt offerings. (Hosea 6:6)

I wanted a coffee, and I didn't want to be anyone's reason to be working on Sunday. I got my desire for a coffee—mediocre though it was—but lots of folks were working on Sunday to satisfy our needs. I quoted Jesus, *"The Sabbath was made for man, not man for the Sabbath...."* (Mark 2:27) but I really didn't believe these words. It felt safe to live by my Sunday rules: always go to church and don't make others work. Was I giving more priority to sacrifices than to love and goodness and the acknowledgment of God?

Not Like the Good Old Days

Angela's birthday was on Tuesday, but because Thursday was *Christian Skate Night* at the local roller rink, we scheduled her party to coincide. As the mother of a new teenager I was to chauffeur and chaperon the group of seven lively young ladies. I rather looked forward to the evening as this particular group of thirteen-year-olds were responsible, well-behaved and wouldn't need much supervision.

As well, I remembered a fondness for roller skating; never mind that I hadn't done it for at least ten years. I assumed roller skating was one of those abilities impossible to lose. Therefore it surprised me somewhat when my 39-year-old body wobbled its way around the rink with hardly a recollection of skills such as turning or stopping. I, who used to do gliding swans and shooting ducks (or whatever those things were called), prudently edged myself over to an off-rink bench to deal with my unforeseen dilemma.

Of course as soon as I sat down Angela came over, inquiring, "Aren't you going to skate?"

"Oh...I'm just taking my time. We've got three hours." Having said that, I felt suddenly depressed.

"Bye, then!" Angela adeptly skated away.

I watched the skaters whiz around for several moments when it occurred to me I had been employing figure skating techniques. Roller skating was different. With restored confidence I returned to the rink to roll with the best of them. I chose a somewhat relaxed, lazy pace, but if anyone had asked me I would have shown them a shooting duck or maybe even a gliding swan. Fortunately no one asked, and it dawned on me as the evening wore on that it must have been my dexterity at ice-skating I remembered. Even so, I was enjoying myself rolling around the rink recalling the skating parties of my teen years, a time when my life was coloured with an ever-present desire for Prince Charming.

Of course the music was different then. In those years before Christian rock, even when a group of Christian young people rented the whole arena, we skated to "Hey, Hey, We're the Monkees," "Yellow Submarine" and "Eight Days a Week."

But what was this I was hearing, here at the *Christian Skate*? "Damned to hell, damned to hell, damned to hell," over and over and over again. Could I be mistaken? A few songs later I heard a refrain that shook me even further, "Sex is a wonderful thing, sex is a wonderful thing." Was I really hearing this? This was Christian music? I was so bewildered I fell flat on my backside. A kind young man helped me up. I stiffly skated off to a bench to rub my sore elbow and continue to contemplate the "Christian" music.

Later when I asked Angela and her friends what the music meant, they informed me that the lyrics were, "May the devil be forever damned to hell," and "Sex is a wonderful thing within the bonds of marriage;" two statements with which I could hardly argue. Still it made me apprehensive to think of my teenage daughter cruising the rink with hormones, no doubt, cruising her body and lyrics such as these cruising her head. My elbow still hurt too. And there was another thought troubling me: *just how much of my belief system was riddled with false assumptions and misinformation?*

> *"I will give you the keys of the kingdom of heaven; whatever you bind on earth will be bound in heaven, and whatever you loose on earth will be loosed in heaven." (Matthew 16:19)*

My ice-skating memories became roller-skating recollections. Even after I had the lyrics to the songs explained, I was still interpreting them the way I first heard them. I do that sort of thing with the Bible as well. When I was a child I thought Matthew 16:19 was about "finding" and "losing." When my Dad found a ball and gave it to me and I lost it again, I could look forward to finding it again in heaven because it had originally been found on earth. It made sense at the time.

How much of the Bible am I interpreting inaccurately?

A 'Short Stay'

As infants both Allison and Amanda needed their tear ducts probed. The difference: Allison had hers done a decade earlier in a small town community without anaesthetics right in the family doctor's office. The doctor directed a thin metal probe into Allison's tear ducts while I held her head and prayed. We were a team. The whole process took about three minutes.

Since then we moved to the big city where an enlightened medical profession realizes the economic danger of possible lawsuits and has adjusted patient care accordingly.

Ten years after Allison's operation, baby Amanda's family doctor referred her to an eye specialist who looked at her eyes, talked about a simple procedure, asked about allergies and asthma, marked my "no's" on a form, then booked her for surgery to take place in three months.

I told him about Allison's three-minute operation. He gasped, "That wasn't done here?"

"No," I admitted.

"It's much too risky. There is a danger of tearing," he explained. Negating the power of prayer, I agreed with him.

On the day before the operation Amanda and I waited patiently to visit the eye specialist who examined her eyes once again and gave us a re-run of the speech he had delivered three months previous. "This is a simple procedure. There is a slight risk with the anaesthetic. Does she have any allergies?"

"No."

"Asthmatic reaction?"

"No."

"Heart disease?"

"No."

Then he sent us on to an anaesthetist (not the one to be at the operation) who weighed her in at 24 pounds and asked about allergies, asthmatic reactions and heart disease. She marked my negative responses on a form.

From there Amanda went for a blood-letting in which two entire tubes of blood were drawn from her little arm. All this and we hadn't even got to the day of the "simple procedure" yet.

The next morning Amanda and I left home promptly at seven. We reported to the "short stay" area of the hospital where Amanda exchanged her clothes for a nightgown. A nurse came to take her temperature and gave her an adult-sized identification bracelet.

For the next hour we hung around the "short stay" area and I wondered why we had been told to arrive so early.

Shortly before nine I carried Amanda through what seemed like a kilometre of corridors to the operating room area where I changed into a green costume complete with paper hat, shoe covers and mask. We waited. The eye specialist/surgeon came. He wrote a prescription for eye drops which I tucked into my green costume pocket. We waited. The anaesthetist came. "Allergies?"

After hearing this question so many times, I was beginning to wonder if maybe Amanda did have allergies, but I answered "no" anyway. Then I was asked still more of the questions I had answered before.

The nurses attached the intravenous, and the anaesthetist put Amanda under a mask. Once Amanda was out, a nurse led me to the change room where I retrieved my clothes and returned to a waiting room.

In a quarter of an hour the surgeon came to inform me, "It went well technically although we met with a lot of resistance, quite a blockage. Don't be concerned if there is slight bleeding from the nose. You have my prescription?" I was nodding until his question about the prescription which, I suddenly realized, I must have discarded with the green costume.

The doctor led me to the nurses' station where he rewrote the prescription. I apologized profusely—somehow I felt someone with the salary of a surgeon shouldn't spend his expensive time re-doing things due to my carelessness. He gave me the prescription again, shook my hand and I thanked him.

The next two hours were spent in recovery and "short stay" with Amanda. She cuddled into my lap snuggling her blanket, sucking her thumb and finger. This must be what they refer to as "quality time."

Given a choice, I would chose three minutes in a small town doctor's office.

> ...a man is not justified by observing the law, but by faith in Jesus Christ. So we, too, have put our faith in Christ Jesus that we may be justified by faith in Christ and not by observing the law, because by observing the law no one will be justified. (Galatians 2:16)

The contrast between the small-town doctor's office of previous years and the modern, worldly wise, big city approach is a picture of the difference between the simplicity of having a relationship with Jesus and the more complicated trying to stay right with God by establishing rituals. Much as I preferred simplicity, I often reasoned my way into complexity. I knew I was saved by grace and obeyed the law out of gratitude. But just as the medical establishment protected itself with anaesthetics, questionnaires and bureaucracy, I measured the security of my salvation by how well I lived. I went to church twice every Sunday; I prayed before and after every meal, and generally felt protected within my adopted guidelines.

A Master Thief

The cashier at the local drug store said, "$26.15 please." She waited impatiently as I dug through my wallet for my credit card. Finally I found the card down between an outdated family picture and my birth certificate. It looked somewhat unfamiliar as I pass it into the drumming fingers of the cashier.

She ran the card through the slot on the cash register and received a "get author" message on the screen.

There was a line of customers forming behind me. The cashier telephoned to get authorization. They put her on hold so she arranged for another cashier to open at another till and told the people behind me that she would be awhile. She punched in some numbers.

Suddenly I realized I had given her my old credit card — the one Marty told me to destroy when he handed me the new Christian Labour Association of Canada (CLAC) one. My CLAC credit card and my driver's license were in the special zippered pocket of my purse where I had slipped these cards after using them at the library instead of my library card which I had left on the spice rack at home. This all came to me in a sudden flash of brilliance.

"I gave you the wrong card!" I said as I slapped down the proper one.

But the cashier didn't appear to hear me. She wouldn't look my way. She wouldn't look at the card on the counter. The line behind me was growing longer. I spoke louder. "Excuse me, excuse me, I gave you the wrong card!" She put her hand up to let me know she couldn't listen to me — she was on the phone. I stopped trying to get her attention.

The other cashier, ten metres away, held up an item and asked, "How much is this?"

Miraculously my cashier was able to answer, "Ask Jane; she's at the back."

That's when, in another flash of brilliant understanding, I realized I was being considered a thief.

My cashier finally got off the line. "I'm sorry, this card is unauthorized," she said as she looked out across the store.

"I know," I babbled. "I gave you the wrong card. My husband applied for new cards and I forgot to destroy...." My explanation faded off into nothingness.

"They want me to send the card in," she said.

"That's okay," I mumbled. It occurred to me to ask her to snip it in half first, but it was obviously a useless card. I figured she wouldn't take advice from me anyway.

She wouldn't even look at me or acknowledge my excuse, but she did pick up my CLAC card. She ran this card through the slot.

"It's okay," she noted. Was that surprise I detected in her voice?

She bagged my items.

"Sorry about that," I murmured.

She accepted my apology with, "That's all right," and focused on the next customer.

I found it most humiliating being considered guilty when I wasn't. It made me wonder how Jesus felt.

The chief priests accused him of many things...But Jesus still made no reply, and Pilate was amazed. (Mark 15:3,5)

Jesus wasn't the least bit guilty. He wasn't even somewhat careless and forgetful as I was with the cards. He, very purposefully, in obedience to His Father went through the humiliation of the cross, being considered guilty when He was totally innocent. He came out the victor because He cared only about pleasing His Father. To be more like Him I have to focus less on what the cashier or the other customers might think and more on pleasing the Father who knows everything—even my heart.

Crime on Our Street

For over a week I had been idly curious about the strange car parked at the end of our block. Every morning as I walked by, I noticed a young fellow in T-shirt and jeans lounging behind the wheel, sipping a cup of take-out coffee. One morning I saw him hand a small package to the driver of another car—suspicious activity, I thought.

I very much wanted to ask the young fellow what he was doing parked at the end of our block, but I never felt quite bold enough.

Then one fine morning as I began my walk, five-year-old, rookie cyclist Michelle asked if she could ride along on her bicycle.

"May I go ahead of you?"

"Stay on the sidewalk," I cautioned.

She wobbled along quite confidently. Then for no apparent reason, her front tire veered completely to the left, into the right taillight of that strange car parked at the end of the block.

The car's red light-cover cracked, crumbling into pieces. The man lounging inside, sprung out of the car, pointed at Michelle and ordered, "Stay right there!"

Michelle burst into tears.

The man got back into his car and spoke into a radio. Several moments later he came around to the rear of the car where sobbing Michelle and I were standing. He smiled. "Do you know this girl?" he asked me.

Devoted mother that I am, I admitted, "She's my girl."

"Unfortunately this car belongs to the Hamilton-Wentworth Police Force. I'm a police officer."

Another car approached and parked nearby. A slightly older fellow, also in jeans and a T-shirt, got out. He had a big amused smile on his face. This was the first policeman's boss. I figured he would waive the whole incident, but no—Michelle had committed a *bona fide* offence under the Highway Traffic Act. They took her full name and address and promised to send a marked police car to our home shortly.

I tried to comfort Michelle as she pushed her bicycle home. "It will be okay," I said. "It was an accident." She continued to sob, pointing at a large piece of taillight which had landed in her bicycle basket. "Take it out," she pleaded.

As soon as we were home she ran upstairs, drew the bedroom curtains tight and crawled into her bed.

Almost an hour later a uniformed officer pulled up in a "real" police car. I went out to meet him.

"She's scared." I told him as I nodded up toward Michelle who was timidly peering out from between the bedroom curtains.

"No reason to be," he assured.

He was a wonderful, friendly officer who had Michelle smiling as he sat across from her at the dining room table recording her crime and using his police radio to get a violation number.

"You know you are not supposed to ride on the sidewalk," he admonished.

"Yes, you can!" said Michelle.

I backed her up, "She's just learning. We really don't want her on the street."

"I don't blame you," he admitted.

On his way out, the policeman promised to send Michelle an Elmer safety kit.

Since then Michelle has become a very careful cyclist and I have spent time wondering about crime on our street.

> But when the kindness and love of God our Savior appeared, he saved us, not because of righteous things we had done, but because of his mercy. He saved us

through the washing of rebirth and renewal by the Holy Spirit... (Titus 3:4–5)

The law told us Michelle was a criminal. She had violated the Highway Traffic Act. The wonderfully friendly uniformed officer (like Jesus) acknowledged her crime, took away the blame and promised her an Elmer safety kit (like the Holy Spirit) to help her deal with the future.

On Becoming 40

As my 40th birthday approached, I discerned this milestone would make it next to impossible to continue identifying with the 24-year-old I once was. This was probably why I wanted to keep the event low-key, maybe even ignore it. Of course Marty who would be 39 for another six months thought we should celebrate with a big party.

I said, "No! Why go through all that fuss and bother to have people come and acknowledge my middle age?" This superior reasoning killed the party idea.

Marty didn't mention it again. Although he did wonder out loud about having a few people over.

"Let's have a party when you turn 40," I bargained. Marty agreed and not another word was said.

Nevertheless, on the eve of my birthday, a few people showed up. Actually the living room was crowded. It looked suspiciously like a party. The guests brought wise-cracking birthday cards and a cake with candles that wouldn't blow out; and some guests even dressed in appropriately out-dated fashion. We had a wonderful time.

The next morning, the morning of my birthday, I found the red maple on the front lawn decorated with balloons and toilet tissue courtesy of thoughtful neighbours. They also planted a sign announcing, "She's 40."

Additional celebrations included visits from both sets of parents. Marty's parents stayed the weekend to watch the metamorphosis take place, and my parents came on the actual birthday to have a look at their middle-aged daughter.

My friend in British Columbia sent a box of *Old Dutch* potato chips. Marty gave me a button that said, "Speak up, I'm 40," and the kids presented a booklet called, "I'd rather be 40 than pregnant." I think it was a hint.

Now that the merry-making is over I'm having a difficult time forgetting my age. As suspected, I can no longer identify with the younger set. I see myself as the person my mother used to be.

The teacher in Ecclesiastes advises:

> *There is a time for everything, and a season for every activity under heaven...I know that there is nothing better for men than to be happy and do good while they live. (Ecclesiastes 3:1,12)*

Surely there is more. I want my life to be meaningful. Why did God put me in this time and this place? What is my purpose?

I want to bloom.

A Prayer With Instant Answers

"Lord, open my eyes to the needs around me and use me." To be honest, part of me didn't really want God to answer that prayer. I had enough to do. On the other hand, the comfortableness of my life was making me uneasy, so I prayed the prayer.

That very Sunday morning, I found myself offering a handful of facial tissues to a bent-up old lady in a wheelchair at the nursing home service sponsored by our church. I saw the sneeze; I watched the lady hopelessly searching her apron pockets. And I knew where the tissue box was because I had absently watched a volunteer worker use it earlier. There—the Lord answered my prayer. "Thank you Lord." But wait, he had more answers.

On Wednesday I heard about a pregnant woman with three little children, a sick husband and a dirty house. If I hadn't prayed the prayer, I know I would have merely felt sorry for that lady, maybe prayed for her and ended my concern there. Instead I organized a house-cleaning party! I don't even like cleaning house or organizing parties for that matter. Afterwards I could say, "Thank you, Lord, for answering my prayer. It was even fun."

That Friday I was on an errand in downtown Hamilton. As I hurried along the sidewalk in one of the less well-to-do areas I noticed a teenage mother coming toward me, carrying a newborn and awkwardly pushing an empty stroller. The stroller kept veering off course. I wondered why she didn't just put the baby in the buggy and push with both hands. As she came closer I noticed the mother's tears. After she passed by I remembered my prayer. The Lord had opened my eyes to the girl's distress. Now, what was I going to do about it? I turned around, caught up to her and asked if she needed help.

"My baby fell and hit his head," she sobbed.

Did she want me to take her to the hospital?

"No," she said, "I just have a few more blocks to go. My boyfriend lives up here. He has a car. He'll drive me."

"May I push the buggy for you?" She let me and blurted out her story. She had been guiding her stroller down the steps outside a store. The wheel wobbled; the stroller toppled, and the baby spilled out onto the sidewalk. He hit his little head on the cement. She showed me the bruise.

I pushed the offending vehicle to the home she indicated. She thanked me and disappeared inside. "Thank you, Lord. You sure do answer prayers efficiently."

> *Each of you should look not only to your own interests, but also to the interests of others. (Philippians 2:4)*

My prayers were readily answered when I prayed in faith according to God's Word. Part of me wants all of life to be like this. Part of me is holding back. If I let go, what would happen to my life? It would be out of my control. Do I trust God enough to let that happen?

Ants

Frequently, ever more frequently, I was seeing ants, big black ants crawling up the brickwork on the front porch, and inside the house they were crawling across the kitchen floor, along the upstairs hallway and around the bathroom sink. Sometimes I let them be. Sometimes I squeezed them into a paper tissue.

I was also finding what looked like tiny crumbs inside my kitchen cupboards. I realized that these were bits of chewed up sawdust after someone informed me my big black ants were no ordinary run-of-the-mill ants: they were carpenter ants. These ants were eating up my home.

Would our insurance replace a house which had been reduced to a pile of sawdust? I wondered. But it wasn't until several very large ants dropped out of the basement office ceiling onto my work area, that I finally declared war.

A neighbour recommended *Green Cross Ant Killer*. I faithfully placed little sticky droplets on windowsills and at doorways. The ants seemed to ignore them.

Rather annoyed, I turned to "Extermination" in the yellow pages. I called the answering services of four different companies. All four companies called me back promptly that same day—as I was preparing supper.

They each offered a different approach. There was the spray-everything-in-sight method; the scientific approach involving discussion, analysis, solution and maintenance; the expensive, "Why not have us chemically treat your lawn as well?" and the natural method which involved leaving food out for the ants to take back to their nests. Prices ranged from

$225 to $350 with three-month, six-month and one-year guarantees, depending on the approach, not the price. The most expensive method had the shortest guarantee.

Needless to say the phone calls left me rather confused. Maybe my accountant husband could sort out this one.

It happened my parents had been invited to help eat the supper I was trying to make between phone calls. I should have asked Dad's advice in the first place. It sounded rather Biblical, "Just watch them yourself." (He didn't actually say "sluggard.") "See where they go. You'll find the nest soon enough."

The next day I tried following Dad's advice—it was cheap and Marty recommended it—but the ants seemed to sense what I was doing. They wandered around in circles until I got bored. This took about a minute and a half.

They also must have sensed my interest in their demise—because they disappeared. Or are they in the dormant stage? There has to be some wisdom here somewhere.

> *Go to the ant, you sluggard; consider its ways and be wise! It has no commander, no overseer or ruler, yet it stores its provisions in summer and gathers its food at harvest. (Proverbs 6:6–8)*

An ant gets a lot done without reasoning or knowing why. It blindly follows a God-given instinct. Sometimes we turn every which way with our problems, but God always has the best answer. We have to trust Him. He can put the answer in us.

A Story of Rachel and Leah

"This is not the fridge I agreed to buy," I said to the two deliverymen as we three stood in the back of their truck examining a scratched and dented appliance.

There had been two of these refrigerators in the store. One was immaculate and the other looked like it had been in a fight with a lift truck. Marty and I had agreed to buy the Rachel, but the store had sent the Leah. The deliverymen knew all about Rachel—they had already delivered her somewhere else.

Now they were asking me to sign a form saying I would accept Leah, dents, scratches and all. I refused so they left with the damaged appliance. I immediately phoned the store.

"Do you have the fridge there?" the man wanted to know.

"No, I sent it back," I said. Did he think I was stupid?

"Well, you should have taken it, and then we could arrange something," he said in all seriousness.

I told him I didn't want a dented scratched appliance for the price of a perfectly good one. The man advised me to talk to Simon who had sold us the fridge and who would be in on Wednesday.

On Wednesday morning I called Simon. He listened to my woes, pleaded ignorance and innocence and asked, "What would you like us to do?"

"Give me the same model without dents."

On Wednesday afternoon Simon called me. He used his best salesman's voice, "Good news, Mrs. den Boer. Well, it's good news for you. We can't get another refrigerator in that model, but we'll give you a fifty dollar discount on this one and we'll remove the dents and scratches."

According to Simon, a service man would come to my home with a replacement door panel and handle. This miracle worker would repair scratches with touch-up paint, and using a dent extractor he would pull out the dents. "It's a powerful suction cup," Simon explained. "Works wonders."

On Thursday the refrigerator arrived once more, complete with dents, nicks and scratches. This time I let it in.

On Friday a repairman showed up. He looked at the fridge.

"I'll order a new handle for you, and we can replace the door panel, but I can't do anything about those dents in the side," he said.

"What about your dent extractor?"

"A what?" he said.

"The salesman told me you had a tool that could pull out dents." I was beginning to feel a wee bit foolish.

The repairman tried very hard not to laugh. He pretended to be engrossed in the refrigerator as he regained his composure.

"You mean there is no such thing?" I asked sheepishly.

"Salesmen," he muttered. "They should go on service calls for a few years."

"Do they do this often?" I asked.

He nodded, "They want to sell refrigerators."

> When the Lord saw that Leah was not loved, he opened her womb, but Rachel was barren. (Genesis 29:31)

The new handle and door panel did wonders for Leah. And the way she was situated next to the bird cage, one really didn't notice the dents in her side. The blemish-free Rachel would have cost fifty dollars more. Discounting the fact that no one likes to be deceived, which was the better deal?

In the Biblical story Jacob obviously thought Rachel far surpassed Leah. When the Lord readily gave Jacob and Leah four sons (including Judah), Jacob still preferred Rachel. Even though Jacob didn't love Leah and had been deceived by his father-in-law into marrying her in the first place, she was chosen by God to be an ancestor of Jesus. God has the ability to work around, through and with all our deceptions and manipulations to achieve His perfect plan. Think how much faster he could work if we would co-operate.

A Good Deed, Indeed!

It began with a phone call from the church hospitality committee, "Could you make supper for John and Gena Vanderlip this Wednesday?"

"Sure," I said without hesitation or reservation. Although we didn't know them very well, our family had been thinking about and praying for the Vanderlips for the past few days. Gena had just had a baby. There had been serious complications—the baby was fine, but mother was feeling pretty feeble.

"I think I'll make my special broccoli with rice dish," I said to myself as I wrote "Cook for J and G" in the Wednesday block on the kitchen calendar.

The week was flying along as usual when one afternoon as I was preparing the family meal, I came across a head of broccoli. "What day is it?" I wondered in panic. A glance at the calendar confirmed my fear—Wednesday had already happened. It was Thursday.

I pulled myself together and got on the phone. It rang and rang. She was probably feeding the baby or maybe resting. Finally Gena answered, and I introduced myself.

"Yes," came the short cold reply.

No doubt the hospitality committee had informed her when and who would be sending meals.

"Oh, Gena, I am so sorry, I was supposed to make your supper yesterday."

"That's okay." She sounded almost forgiving. "When we finally got over it, we had oatmeal instead."

I apologized all over the place, and she forgave me a million times, but nothing could change the deed not done.

As an exclamation mark to my sin of omission, that very evening at our small Bible study group we happened to discuss:

> *For we are God's workmanship created in Christ Jesus to do good works, which God prepared in advance for us to do. (Ephesians 2:10)*

If the Vanderlip Wednesday night meal was a good work God had prepared in advance for me to do, why didn't He remind me to do it? Maybe I was too busy doing my own stuff to hear about His stuff. Maybe I'm not tuned in. I wonder how many other good works I've left undone.

I know good deeds don't get us to heaven—that's a gift. But I do want to live out God's purposes in my life.

More Precious than Gold

Marty and I finally found the courage and a free Saturday to cover our ugly yellow and red scarred floors in the kitchen and hallways with the lovely peel-and-stick blue floral tiles we had purchased on sale a year before.

Of course we should have sat the children down and explained this was a don't-bother-us project, but we didn't. So our children invited neighbourhood friends over. Soon there were ten people in the house and eight of them were children without adult supervision.

Inevitably each of them had to use the washroom at least twice. To do this they had to navigate around the kitchen furniture in outlying rooms and past us kneeling on the kitchen floor. Each passing child was full of questions.

"What about this corner? Are you going to leave it like this? When will you be done? How come it isn't straight here?"

Certainly the children should have been astute enough to feel the tension, to pick up the stay-out-of-our-face message we were exuding. Obviously they weren't quite that clever, so I yelled at them, chased them out of the house and locked the door.

Of course fifteen minutes later we had to find them and feed them, but they had taken the hint and promptly disappeared after lunch. That is all except two-year-old Amanda. She decided to help. She moved tiles and tools around and generally stood on the very spot we were working.

"Get her out of here!" Marty commanded through clenched teeth. I put Amanda to bed even though she had already spent most of her morning there.

No sooner was I back on my knees, head bowed, totally engrossed in cutting a tile to fit precisely around a door frame when the door bell rang.

"Are you going to answer that?" Marty asked.

"No!" I said, intuitively sure it was a child, probably one of ours.

Marty who operates on less intuition and more common sense, decided to go to the door.

I blushed to see my parents. They were touring the countryside, celebrating their wedding anniversary. They were also returning Amanda's shoes, the ones we had left behind on our last visit.

Of course we invited them in and offered them refreshments and looked at their pictures.

But they must have noticed our eyes darting back to the floor because they left within 20 minutes without even catching a glimpse of a precious grandchild. We were on our knees again as the door closed behind them.

At five we rounded up our children, shared a simple meal and sent them off for baths and bed. Finally at eleven o'clock that evening, silly with fatigue, we finished.

Did you ever wonder why God created the world and everything in it *before* adding the crowning work—his children?

> "*A new command I give you: Love one another. As I have loved you, so you must love one another.*" (John 13:34)

As I contemplated the job, I appreciated the new floor of flowered tiles and felt a pride in our careful workmanship, but had a nagging apprehension about mistreating the people in my life worth more to me than even a floor of pure gold.

Very often I focus on the project, the program, the wonderful *thing* I am doing for God—while relationships suffer. My floor may be blooming, but I'm not—yet.

A Thorn in the Side

"I have come to the definite conclusion that musical ability is not an inborn talent but an ability which can be developed. Any child, properly trained, can develop musical ability..."

Shinichi Suzuki

These words found in the introduction of my son's music book have left me in a quandary. Either the renowned Mr. Suzuki (of "Suzuki Method" violin and piano studies fame) didn't know what he was talking about (which I doubt) or I could have been properly trained (which I also doubt).

When I was a small, malleable child I assumed I could sing. Reality struck in Grade 1 when my teacher was compelled to ask me to mouth the words at the Christmas concert. She was a sensitive teacher; she made me feel proud to be the one to make this special silent contribution to a successful program.

In Grade 2 my report card was plastered with A's except for the row of C's next to the word "music."

The only red blot that ever appeared on my report card happened in Grade 4 when the music mark was based entirely on ability to sing. I got 38.

In Grade 7 every student was required to sing a solo to the class. Along with several boys, I balked. We were threatened with an alternative; write out the words and music of a hymn. I jumped at the opportunity, imagining myself with a perfect music mark for once. I would transcribe the entire hymn book sooner than subject my classmates to my sad attempt at making my voice sing. They were not sensitive classmates.

The threatened alternative was a bluff, and in the end the class suffered through my rendition of "Just As I Am without One Plea."

As an adult I mouth the hymns in church. I do let my voice out now and then, but Marty rescues the congregation with a quick poke in my side. I thank him for this.

I admit my musical history does not involve any serious attempt at proper training. But then who would have the time or talent to train someone who finds it impossible to sing "Happy Birthday" the same way twice or who can't hear the difference between one melody and the next unless there are words involved?

My gut feeling is that not even Mr. Suzuki could have trained me successfully. I believe I am musically retarded or, in modern language, "musically challenged" beyond hope this side of heaven. Is there a support group for people like me?

It's not that I want to change. I believe this thorn in my side is a blessing. It keeps me humble. Secretly I think God created me this way to save me from a vain singing career. Such is the philosophy I have built around my musical inadequacy. I'm good at finding a way to like myself just as I am.

> *To keep me from becoming conceited because of these surpassingly great revelations, there was given me a thorn in my flesh, a messenger of Satan, to torment me. (2 Corinthians 12:7)*

Paul's thorn in the side also kept him from becoming conceited. The similarity between my thorn and Paul's stops there. He had to deal with constant demonic attack—"a messenger of Satan to torment." He was continually being mobbed, stoned and thrown out of town. Difficulties and persecutions followed him everywhere. In that light, being musically challenged is a mere prickle.

Tough Love

If I were a car my practical husband jokingly said he would not hesitate to abandon me in favour of a working model. I thought of this as "tough love"—I hoped it was love.

It all came down to my repeated backaches and a broken promise. About two or three times each year my family suffered through my immobilizing back pain. Sleeping on a lumpy bed, pulling on a sock, bending over to pick up a toy, lifting Amanda onto the change table; any of these things could possibly send a jab of agony into my lower back. Then the muscles would tighten up around the pain and I became an invalid.

Well, the family was sick of this routine. They were under the impression that if I did abdomen-strengthening exercises faithfully every day, as I promised, I would never have another backache. They were possibly right.

I made the exercise promise at a low point in my life. At the time I was stretched out across the seat in the back of the van watching the rain stream down the windows. We were on the way home from an interrupted family camping holiday. My back was the reason we were going home four days early. Needless to say I wasn't anywhere close to being nominated "Mother of the Year." Even the rain appeared to be my fault.

At this abyss of my existence, I promised to do exercises for five minutes every day until I turned 65. I managed to break the promise after two months. After that, my family showed a decided lack of sympathy when it came to my backaches.

This particular bout of back pain could be traced to the chilly March morning I woke up without any blankets on — they were all on Marty's side of the bed. My lumbar muscles had tied themselves into knots while I innocently slept. When I stood I resembled the Leaning Tower of Pisa. Somehow, I wishfully expected my family to pamper me to health, tripping over each other to see who could be the best servant. This didn't happen. They simply walked around me hinting that I was to blame for my predicament.

Even my own mother, who wisely stopped giving me direct advice when I entered puberty, let me know she was putting her 72-year-old body through a half-hour Jane Fonda exercise routine every morning while Dad made breakfast.

She told me this as I sat stiffly in her living room trying not to think about the pain involved in moving. This was another low point at which I fell into another promise, "As soon as this backache gets better, I'm going to exercise five minutes every day. If my Mom can do 30 minutes, surely I can do five," I reasoned.

> *What has been will be again, what has been done will be done again; there is nothing new under the sun. (Ecclesiastes 1:9)*

"This time I really am going to do the exercises—forever." Promises and promises and trying and trying—it's all a lot of human effort and exactly what the book of Ecclesiastes talks about. For God's view on this we might as well go directly to the conclusion of the matter found in the last few verses of that book.

> *Now all has been heard; here is the conclusion of the matter: Fear God and keep his commandments, for this is the whole duty of man. For God will bring every deed into judgment, including every hidden thing, whether it is good or evil. (Ecclesiastes 12:13–14)*

Spring and Cleaning

Every spring the robins build their nests, the daffodils pop up, the tulips bloom and women everywhere clean their houses from top to bottom—or at least that's what Marty believes. He wonders why spring doesn't happen at our house.

Oh, the grass turns green, and soon he's mowing the lawn every week; the daffodils bloom, and I canvas for the Cancer Society; but spring and cleaning are two words I have a hard time putting together.

Some years I tell myself—and Marty—that I'm waiting to begin on a perfect spring morning. Then I will be able to fling all the windows open and hang out the bedding (an essential part of Marty's idea about spring cleaning).

Yet the longer I wait for a fine spring day the more unlikely I'll want to spend it indoors cleaning when I could be outdoors enjoying.

Some years I'm too pregnant to clean; some years I have a backache, and some years we simply move. This year we're not moving, I'm not pregnant, I don't have a backache and my house is noticeably gritty. I hate it when that happens.

Marty mentions the grime as much as he dares; I'm very touchy on the subject. But knowing my house is dirty is slightly more painful than cleaning it, so this year I am actually spring cleaning.

For inspiration I've been asking friends and acquaintances about their traditions and habits. A few admitted that they enjoy this chore. One lady said cleaning is one of her favourite things to do. One friend is so efficient she does her spring cleaning in February and fall-cleaning in June.

But most people I talked to either dislike spring cleaning or hate it. Some do it anyway. Some don't. Some scrub walls, floors and everything in sight. Others would rather paint over the dirt. Some make it a family weekend project because both partners work outside the home full-time.

Some people can do their entire house in a week. I haven't been inspired to that point, but I have decided to dedicate a weekly morning to the chore. This is my fifth week and I've done the kitchen (but not inside the cupboards), the washrooms, the hallways, and one bedroom. I may be through by Christmas.

> *I will sprinkle clean water on you, and you will be clean; I will cleanse you from all your impurities and from all your idols. I will give you a new heart and put a new spirit in you; I will remove from you your heart of stone and give you a heart of flesh. (Ezekiel 36:25–26)*

My heart could use a good scrub. There are cobwebs in the prayer room and the Bible study area. The worship room is filled with all sorts of distracting trivia, while the other rooms are strewn with selfishness, pride and discontent. I prayed for help. So now in addition to my morning per week spring cleaning, I'm planning to spend an hour a day in private devotions with the Lord.

It's a plan. I tend to wonder which will get cleaned up first—my heart or my house. I have a suspicion both are ongoing projects.

Training My Children

Sometimes I think one of the reasons God has given us Amanda is to allow me another try at toilet training. Up to now I have been a dismal failure in this area. Angela, Allison, Paul and Michelle all eventually graduated to underwear, but their mother had next to nothing to do with convincing them it was the way to go.

Neither reasoning, psychology, cajoling, begging nor out-and-out bribery worked with any of the children. I seriously considered teaching them to diaper themselves as a simple alternative.

Allison actually had the wherewithal to out-reason me. I found her three-year-old self in the washroom one day. She was holding her doll over the toilet, talking to it in a motherly instructive way. Then she noticed me watching and she explained, "Mommy, my dolly is going to do it on the toilet."

"Is she?" I asked hopefully.

She looked thoughtful and shook her little head. "No," she said, "no she's not."

"Why not?"

"Because her mommy wants her to."

At this point my friend Betty took over. She invited Allison to visit for the afternoon. She put her in a roomful of dolls and doll furniture which Betty's own daughter had outgrown. Over the course of the afternoon Betty explained to Allison that everything in the room could be hers if only she would change her ways.

Allison spent a wonderful afternoon with the dolls, the doll bed, the little highchair, the purses, the clothes and the pretend food. Betty reported high hopes for success.

Allison also reported, "Mommy, Mrs. Hummy thinks I'm going to do it on the toilet."

She didn't get the toys. She waited to make the change in her own good time, a half year later.

Now Amanda, who is almost three, is at the crossroad. She is just as smart, bright, stubborn and impossible. I'm not doing any better with her than I did with the others.

Amanda's training has become a family project. If only she will use the facilities: Marty will take her to the donut shop; Angela will take her to the library; Grandma will let her sleep over; and I will give her candy, ice cream, fancy underwear, a new tricycle, a mountain bike, a sports car. Did I say that? Does she have the upper hand?

> *You were taught, with regard to your former way of life, to put off your old self, which is being corrupted by its deceitful desires; to be made new in the attitude of your minds; and to put on the new self, created to be like God in true righteousness and holiness.(Ephesians 4:22–24)*

Training my children to use the toilet instead of sitting in their personal messes has been a major frustration for me. They each had their own approach, yet they all finally chose underwear over diapers. The deck is stacked in my favour. I just have to be patient.

Possibly God has a similar frustration training me to recognize and flush my messes. Logically, doing things His way would be best. I'm glad He lets me choose (I wouldn't want him to force me) and I'm glad He is patient.

A Life-Changing Challenge

"Try it for just a week," said my friend as she handed me some books on prayer. I wanted to improve my haphazard devotional life which consisted of a quick prayer here and there, and devotions with the family at mealtimes when my mind often wandered.

I had tried sitting down with my Bible during the day, but a child, the telephone or the door would inevitably interrupt. I also tried praying before going to sleep, but I would usually go to sleep before praying.

My friend suggested I start my day early with one hour of prayer and Bible reading.

The books she gave me were filled with helpful suggestions. Begin by praising God. Use the Psalms. Write your prayer requests in a notebook. Write down answers. Read something from the Old Testament, something from the New Testament and something from Proverbs. Summarize what you have read and write it down. Write down verses that speak to you.

Yet for me, getting up early would be the same as turning water into wine or floating an axe-head. I am not a morning person.

Then a suggestion by a Korean author did turn my water into wine. He said, "Ask the Lord to wake you."

If I asked God to open my eyes, I could hardly close them again. It would be like inviting a friend over and then slamming the door in her face.

I tried; I spent the hour with the Lord for a week, and three months later I'm still doing it. The Lord always knows exactly when to wake me. Without fail He gets me up an hour before interruptions by the family. It might be 5:30, 5:55, 6:00 or even 7:00.

As a result I am more peaceful, have more time for my kids, feel more efficient at my work, and care more about others.

When I think about it, spending time with the Lord for one hour each morning is the best deal around. Where else can I get free expert advice from a top consultant? I praise the Lord for His greatness, thank Him for all He does for me, admit my mistakes and listen to His timely direction.

> *Jesus replied, "If anyone loves me, he will obey my teaching. My Father will love him, and we will come to him and make our home with him."(John 14:23)*

Of course life goes on. The basement floods when the laundry tub overflows because I leave a sock in the sink. Three-year-old Amanda is not toilet-trained yet. Allison flicks a yo-yo in the kitchen and shatters the light shade. Marty's dad delivers six bags of ripe chicken manure to spread on our garden and flowerbeds (to the despair of my pregnant neighbour). Things such as these still happen, but they don't irritate me quite like before. Although, I have to admit my reaction to the chicken manure (once again) wasn't absolutely angelic.

Overall I feel more empathy for the needs of others. Somehow, I've got more love to give. I never imagined spending an hour each day with the Lord would make me feel this good.

I'm beginning to know the One I admired from a distance.

I Blush to Tell You This

Early each morning of our camping holiday as the sun was just pulling itself over the horizon, I would slip out of our tent, grab the Bible and head over to the rocks for my hour of morning devotions.

Up on the rocks among the trees in Muskoka at 6 a.m. is the perfect place and time to commune with the Lord; that is, unless a night rain drenches the rocks.

Thus on one rather damp morning instead of sitting on wet rocks (slapping mosquitoes), I strolled along the road praying. I carried my Bible with me. The cool morning air made me grateful for the bulky green sweatshirt I had pulled on over my other clothes. As I wandered, the quiet country road led me past "Group of Seven" scenes: rocks, trees, bushes, water and muskeg. I thanked the Lord for the beautiful wild country.

My prayer changed abruptly where the road dipped through a patch of muskeg. That was where the flies attacked. First one, then two and then a whole swarm of them, circled my head, dive-bombing my face and hair. These were relentless little invaders with broad triangular wings and striped bodies—bigger than houseflies, smaller than horseflies, and peskier than both.

The flies had me swinging my arms, swatting wildly at the air and running. You might call it fly-induced aerobics. My prayer was reduced to a single plea, "Lord, get these flies out of my life."

Because they seemed only interested in my head, it occurred to me to take off my sweatshirt and tie it up around my head into a turban. Now the flies could buzz and dive-bomb as much as they pleased; I couldn't hear them as my ears were covered; I couldn't even see them because they didn't bother coming down past my strange lopsided turban.

Finally, back at my devotions, I thought I would read a Psalm, a praising one. As I opened my Bible I noticed a pick-up truck driving up behind me. Immediately I felt embarrassed — but not because I was wearing a large green bundled-up shirt on my head with a swarm of flies buzzing around it. I had actually forgotten that for the moment. I was embarrassed because I was walking along the road reading the Bible—God's Word.

So I discreetly closed the book and continued walking nonchalantly along. Three vehicles—two trucks and a car—whizzed by one after the other on that otherwise lonely, quiet road.

A rooster couldn't have crowed louder. I instantly realized what a fool I was. I felt totally stupid and ashamed of myself.

"If anyone is ashamed of me and my words, the Son of Man will be ashamed of him when he comes in his glory..." (Luke 9:26a)

Like Peter, I asked God to forgive me. He did. Now that I'm spending time with the Lord, the conviction, repentance and forgiveness process has become essential. I don't want anything to separate me from Him.

I am still puzzled as to why walking along the road reading the Bible embarrassed me so.

A Pig and a Whistle

This year for the first time ever our family spent a whole day at Canada's Wonderland. We left three-year-old Amanda with a baby-sitter. Of course she protested; three-year-olds don't like to miss things. I pacified her with the promise of a present.
"We'll bring you something. What would you like?"
"Bring me a little pig!" she said.
"Okay," I readily agreed, gambling there would be such a thing available at an amusement park.
"And a whistle," she added hopefully.
Amanda likes pigs. Of all the unique and wonderful animals in God's world she has chosen the pig as her very favourite.
At Wonderland we came across a two-dollar carved wooden pig about the size of Amanda's hand. It was painted pink with black markings.
"Not much of a toy," remarked Marty.
Nevertheless I noted the location of that pig. It might be our only choice.
Later in the day while the others were spending an hour in their bathing suits at Splash Works, I took some time to search for the perfect pig and a whistle.
The whistle was easy. I found a pink plastic flute for 56 cents at the first souvenir stand. The pig was another story. Sales people sent me from one area to the next. There were cats, sheep, bears and horses, but no pigs.
Several salespeople suggested I win a pig, a disagreeable idea that nevertheless sent me wandering among booths noting

the prizes for shooting targets, breaking balloons, flipping quarters onto plates, and rolling dice.

I stopped at a stall for tossing baseballs into milk cans. There, before my eyes, sat a cuddly pink pig, four times the size of Amanda. She would love it. The sign said, "one toss $2 or three tries for $5." Although the milk can had a very narrow opening I thought I had a chance; at home I'm always tossing tin cans and plastic bottles into the blue recycling box at twice that distance.

I handed the nice young man two dollars. He handed me a baseball; my heart sank: the ball was Styrofoam. O well, you never know, maybe an angel would guide it to its destination.

The young man suggested I put a backward spin on the ball. I concentrated on the task. A boy approached, "How do you do this?" I told him and then refocused as he watched intently. When I finally let the ball go it missed the can entirely. The boy walked away in disgust and I trudged over to buy the little wooden pig.

The next morning Amanda greeted us with, "Did you buy me a pig and a whistle?"

Paul blew out a little tune, then handed her the plastic flute.

She hugged it and blew it and smiled.

"And the pig?" she asked.

Angela pulled out the little block pig from behind her back saying, "What do you tell *Mommy*?" She emphasized *Mommy* so there would be no mistaking who to thank.

Amanda's delighted face fell. She burst into tears. She wailed and wailed and wailed.

Once she gained control of herself she let us know she had a soft, cuddly pig in mind. I knew that, but I had been intent on keeping my promise.

> *"Woe to you Pharisees, because you give God a tenth of your mint, rue and all other kinds of garden herbs, but you neglect justice and the love of God. You should have*

practiced the latter without leaving the former undone."
(Luke 11:42)

What I did to keep my promise to my daughter is deserving of a "woe to you." I fulfilled my promise as an obligation, making sure my gift fell into the definition of "a little pig," and not at all as an act of love with the intention of delighting my daughter. Offering to take her shopping for a little pig would have been much more loving.

Lord, help me.

A Fake Fireplace

I was just putting the casserole supper into the oven when the phone rang.

"Marian, it's Daina. How flexible are you in the next little while?"

"Pretty flexible," I said, thinking Daina was calling about a newsletter she wanted done.

"There's a networking dinner at The Old Mill. I would like you to be my guest. I'll pick you up in ten minutes."

Dutch as I am, I found it difficult to turn down a free dinner at a classy restaurant, no matter how good my own casserole.

I hung up the phone, bounded upstairs, stripped out of my jeans and sweatshirt, hopped into the shower and ten minutes later I was at the door in my best outfit, the epitome of a businesswoman.

I left a few supper instructions with Angela; and saying goodbye to the children and household routine, I stepped into Daina's sporty white car with the sun roof and fancy cup holder. I didn't even notice my puzzled husband turn into the driveway as we sped off.

There were about 80 women at this "power" business dinner. Everyone was "networking" with a passion. I met accountants, real estate agents, an optometrist, an artist, a printer, communications specialists, health specialists and Susan, who sat directly across from me.

"I'm going to be a world-class motivational speaker," she said as she handed me her business card and a slick brochure from the California company she represented.

"Must be New Age," I thought as I slipped her material into the networking file folder I had received at the door.

The very next day Susan called me at home, "I wonder if we could network further over coffee? Did you get a chance to read the brochure?"

I had. It was all about making dreams come true. It talked about inspiring, empowering and transforming lives without hinting how.

"I found the brochure rather vague," I said. "You see I'm a Christian and...."

"So am I!" she exclaimed.

With that, I invited her to coffee at my home. I could always use some motivation. Then again if Susan happened to be a Christian charmed by hokey New Age stuff it was my duty to rescue her, I reasoned.

Susan came with a pile of tapes and booklets and assured me the ideas behind this dynamic program were biblical. Her company simply felt it best not to mention God or Jesus. They didn't want to alienate a large portion of their potential market—those who don't want anything to do with Christianity.

She left the material with me for the weekend. I spent five hours listening to the tapes and reading the booklets. She was right: most of the ideas were based on biblical principles. And they were very motivating. I decided to become the greatest writer of all time.

On the other hand, I was being told I had within me the power to do anything, and I personally deserved the best of everything.

> *Do not be carried away by all kinds of strange teachings. It is good for our hearts to be strengthened by grace, not by ceremonial foods, which are of no value to those who eat them. (Hebrews 13:9)*

Anyone can take the laws and the teachings of the Bible and work them. They are solid good teachings. Even if we don't acknowledge God as the Creator and Jesus as our Saviour, we can work His true principles to major in external perishing things, and even become hugely successful by worldly standards, but the whole exercise is absolutely of no eternal benefit. Biblical principles without Jesus are like a cheap fake fireplace—fake flame, and no heat.

Curing an Irritating Habit

Allison had a problem. Or rather I had a problem—she didn't see it as a problem at all. She was perfectly content to drop her un-rinsed toothbrush on the bathroom counter after each use.

At least twice a day I would mindlessly pick up her toothbrush, rinse it and hang it in a holder with the rest of the toothbrushes. Then I would wipe the counter.

I suppose I was grateful she was brushing her teeth. Then it occurred to me that this was a routine that I really should not be doing, for in doing it I was inadvertently training up a slob.

I resorted to nagging. Every time I saw the brush on the counter, I would immediately confront Allison, "Put your toothbrush in the holder." If she happened to be out I would write myself a reminder to tell her. She took the nagging in stride. She always obeyed me immediately, but the next time she brushed her teeth she would again leave her toothpaste-covered brush wherever it landed.

It didn't seem to make any difference to her that she could save herself time, and me aggravation, if she simply set her toothbrush in the holder after using it. I like to think she wanted to put it away in the first place but had more important things on her mind while absent-mindedly brushing her teeth.

Two weeks of futile nagging drove me to try a more creative approach. "Allison, if I find your messy toothbrush on the counter one more time I am going to soap it."

She raised an eyebrow and smiled nervously.

I didn't have to wait long to attempt my new tactic. She happened to be in the vicinity when I discovered the offending brush. "I'm going to soap it," I warned. She was quick to stop me.

Allison was in school the next time I found her toothbrush lying in a puddle of water conveniently beside the soap dish. I'll admit I took adverse pleasure in rubbing that toothbrush across the bar of soap before hanging it neatly in the holder.

It was two whole days before I found the brush on the counter again. I rubbed it across the bar of soap again and again the next day and yet again.

Allison never said a word. I was just beginning to think she had developed a taste for soap—when I brushed my teeth, and "ppweth." I had a mouth full of suds before I realized my toothbrush had been soaped. Ugh! Yuk! How could anyone do something so mean as to soap a toothbrush? I was almost sorry I had resorted to such a cruel tactic. On the other hand, now at least I knew the soap was doing its job. A person surely would change more than a simple habit to avoid those bitter soapy suds.

I confidently approached Allison, "So how does your toothbrush taste lately?"

She smiled, "Not so good, but it's very clean."

I never had to soap her toothbrush again.

> *Since they hated knowledge and did not choose to fear the Lord, since they would not accept my advice and spurned my rebuke, they will eat the fruit of their ways and be filled with the fruit of their schemes. (Proverbs 1:29–31)*

As a dutiful parent, I went from overlooking, to pointing out, to reminding, to suggesting a punishment, to warning, to actually punishing. I think God works in much the same way, although I don't think He relishes implementing the punishment; He is love. I want to be more like Him.

Things are Never What They Seem

I don't know what made me think I had the time or talent to prepare a turkey for the high school staff and student dinner, but being in a generous mood I submitted my name and willingness. What's to cooking a turkey? You pop it into the oven and baste it every half hour. Then when your house starts to smell really good you know it's ready.

Two days before the dinner, someone from the school called, "Your turkey is here waiting for you." Why had I assumed someone would bring it to me?

I drove over to get the bird. It was huge—bigger than my bread box. It came with a memorandum thanking me for graciously consenting to do what I was doing, a foil roasting pan, half a dozen eggs, a bunch of celery, a small plastic bag of dried sage, a large onion, a recipe for stuffing a five-pound turkey, and instructions for roasting a twenty-pound bird. This project seemed to be taking on the dimensions of a high school math problem.

The next day after chauffeuring Paul and Michelle to piano lessons and shopping for weekly groceries, I finally got around to the turkey. It was still partially frozen. As it creaked and cracked like a backyard ice rink I struggled to extract the neck and giblets.

I popped the stuffed turkey into the oven shortly after lunch. Then I immediately sped off to collect Angela and Allison for orthodontist appointments. We were only three minutes late. By the time I got back home the bird was in need of serious basting.

At 6:30 that evening at the five-hour mark, the suggested cooking time for a twenty-pound bird, the house was smelling pretty good. I asked Marty to lift the steaming brown-crusted turkey out of the oven.

The hot bird was sitting in the roasting pan in two inches of grease, but it was time to leave for the grade school Christmas concert which I wasn't about to miss. I left with a slight sense of anxiety.

When I got back to the turkey at 10:30 my first task was to scoop out the soggy greasy stuffing. I spent some time doctoring this with dry bread crumbs and flavoured croutons. Almost satisfied with the stuffing I turned to making the gravy—an art I have never fully mastered.

Shortly after 11 p.m. I was ready to slice the turkey. The first four slices looked good—delicate, white meat. The next slice held a distressing pink tint. As I continued to cut I came to the realization that five hours did not cook this turkey.

I sliced up the entire pink bird. Then I threw everything into a roasting pan, covered it and shoved it back in the oven. By 1:30 a.m. the meat looked brown. I didn't bother tasting it.

That morning Marty delivered Angela, the stuffing, gravy and sliced meat to school.

Angela came home mid-afternoon muttering, "I couldn't even eat the stupid turkey."

"Why not?" I asked apprehensively envisioning trays of meat condemned by the banqueters—overcooked, inedible, too dry.

"Guess?" she said in that voice teenagers reserve for dim-witted parents.

I didn't want to guess. I braced myself for the worst, "Well, tell me."

"My teeth," she said. "I couldn't eat because of these stupid elastics the orthodontist put on my teeth."

I don't think she understood or appreciated my sigh of relief.

Now we see but a poor reflection as in a mirror; then we shall see face to face. Now I know in part; then I shall know fully, even as I am fully known. And now these three remain: faith, hope and love. But the greatest of these is love. (1 Corinthians 13:12–13)

Things aren't always what they seem. It seemed simple to cook a turkey—it wasn't. The bird seemed cooked in five hours—it wasn't. Angela seemed upset with the meat—she wasn't. My five fallible senses need help. Often in life we make assumptions and reach conclusions, logical or illogical according to what we know or think we know. But we only "*know in part.*" The way to make it through graciously is with faith, hope and love.

To Soar Like an Eagle

"Our Christian elementary school is celebrating its 40th anniversary this year," said the long-distance voice on the telephone one September evening. "We're wondering if you could be one of several former students to speak at the celebration in May?"

I was flattered. It felt good to be picked. Without thinking, I said "yes" to the voice on the telephone. I assumed she would send me a program when the arrangements were finalized.

Shortly after hanging up I realized I held a rather dim view of my elementary Christian school days. I could remember my first day of Christian education. There I was, wearing my new glasses, a shy stranger enrolled for the final term of Grade 3 among all those kids who knew each other.

I could remember receiving the strap in the furnace room—twice: in Grade 4 for saying uncomplimentary things about my teacher, and in Grade 5 for supposedly mouthing bad words at the principal. I could remember looking forward to summer holidays and longing for them to go on forever.

Why had the anniversary committee chosen me? And, why, oh why, had I so impulsively said yes?

I imagined the committee was planning a banquet involving a parade of speakers. Maybe, as one of many speeches, mine wouldn't have to be profound. I could always come up with something light and corny.

That Christmas, sitting in my parents' living room back home, I idly watched my dad rooting through a desk drawer. After several minutes of rummaging he pulled out a pink sheet.

"I saved this for you," he said without explanation. At the top of the sheet was a flying eagle beside an excerpt from Isaiah 40:31 ...*but those who hope in the Lord will renew their strength. They will soar on wings like eagles...* This was the theme verse for my elementary school's anniversary.

I read below the eagle, "The first day of school this fall marked the beginning of the 40th year of operation for our Christian school. During those years...." I scanned down the page. My eyes fell on the name "Beekman." It kind of jumped out at me, being my maiden name and all. I read, "The main speaker will be Marian (Beekman) den Boer."

"Main speaker?"

I read on, "May 7: Join us at the church for a 'praise and worship' service."

"A praise and worship service!"

Later that afternoon Marty echoed my thoughts, "You can't be corny at a praise and worship service."

Still later, Marty was outside shovelling snow when who should drive by but an anniversary committee member. She stopped to chat. Marty asked, "Do you know what you are doing asking Marian to speak? She writes better than she speaks." (Marty knows me well.)

> ...*but those who hope in the Lord will renew their strength. They will soar on wings like eagles... (Isaiah 40:31)*

Perhaps it had something to do with my excellent elementary school education, but I actually started to look forward to the anniversary celebration. My hope was in the Lord. He would give me the strength to soar like an eagle—I certainly couldn't do it on my own.

On May 7th the Lord proved true to his Word. I delivered a memorized speech as sparkling and witty as anything I've ever written. There's even a video but I haven't had the courage to watch it.

Just as eaglets are pushed out of the nest by the mother eagle who then swoops to their rescue, I was pushed beyond my comfort zone into a place where I had to rely on the Lord. It was exhilarating. I want more.

Loving Your Neighbours

You could see the snow visibly melt under the powerful rays of the sun, but the kids of the neighbourhood didn't have time to consider snow. They had to be running, jumping, climbing, crawling—constantly moving. Each child contrived his own ritual in celebration of this first warm spring day.

Paul whacked at various parts of the house with his hockey stick.

"Paul, stop beating up the house," I said. "It's not ours anymore." (We had recently sold our home.)

Six-year-old Jason from next door twisted his hockey stick blade down into the middle of our front lawn.

"Jason, stop digging up the grass."

"What grass? It's mud."

"Well, stop doing that," I said between clenched teeth. I watched him wipe the muddy blade up against a maple tree where no doubt the next kid would be leaning if only for a second.

"Get off that little trike!" I hollered at Michelle, now nine, who was sitting on the brand new tricycle that belonged to a two-year-old neighbour.

"I don't have all my weight on it," she said innocently.

"Off!" I commanded.

Then I noticed Jack pulling Paul up the street in our wagon: "Guys, guys don't treat the wagon that way. You'll break the axles."

"What way?"

"Twisting it up and down the curbs like that."

They shrugged their shoulders and abandoned the wagon.

"Michelle," I nagged on, "don't roller skate through puddles. Your wheels will get rusty."

"Oh?" she said looking puzzled.

I walked over to my neighbour who was standing on his driveway, barbecuing pork chops.

"You know," I said, "every spring it's the same. You have to re-train the kids. They don't seem to remember anything. You have to tell them not to beat up the house or dig up the lawn or rust up their roller skates or...."

"Marian," he interrupted sympathetically, "are you having a hard day?"

I was amazed at his perception.

"Am I having a hard day? Let me tell you about my day...." I told him how I had flooded the basement doing a load of laundry. Someone (probably me) had left a rag in the laundry tub so the soapy, washing-machine water filled up the tub and spilled over onto the floor and into the office.

I had spent a good part of my morning lifting the office carpet which meant moving a heavy oak desk and pulling apart a packed four-drawer file cabinet. I mistakenly lifted the second drawer of the cabinet by the file hanger apparatus and spend the next twenty minutes sorting out my husband's T-to-Z clients.

My neighbour listened to my woes or at least some of them. I spared him details about my achy neck, my interrupted devotions and the money argument with Marty at breakfast.

I did tell him that after months of shopping for a bigger home in an affordable price range, we finally found one; but I was having qualms. I didn't want to trade neighbourhoods. That's what was really bothering me.

I don't remember exactly what my neighbour said, but pretty soon I was laughing at myself. It's easy to love your neighbours when you have nice ones.

> "Which of these three do you think was a neighbour to the man who fell into the hands of robbers?" The expert in the law replied, "The one who had mercy on him." Jesus told him; "Go and do likewise." (Luke 11:36–37)

Who was being a neighbour in my situation? According to the parable of the Good Samaritan, my neighbour was. He had mercy on me. He didn't judge me or tell me to stop ruining a perfect spring day with my nagging and complaining. He simply listened to my woes, got to the root of my problem and had me laughing at myself. That's the kind of neighbour I want to be.

The Most Delicious Ice-cream Sundae Imaginable

"O Mom, you'd think they'd just invented the game, the way you carry on." Try as she might, my teenage daughter who is always on guard against eccentric behaviour (especially her mother's) couldn't curb my enthusiasm. The possibility of winning a game was all I talked about. I was a women obsessed.

Our neighbours, Jack and Jill, had just mounted a basketball hoop on their garage. Jill had challenged me to win a game of 21. She was an expert. She'd been on her high-school basketball team 18 years ago. According to my hairdresser who had attended school with her, five-foot-three-inch Jill was a champ.

My own experience on the basketball court happened 27 years back when I took a few weeks of mandatory basketball in physical education class. I hadn't even heard of 21.

The rules of the game are simple. You chalk up two points for each successive, successful free throw from a designated line and one point for netting the ball on your opponent's rebound. A one-pointer gets you to the free-throw line. Twenty-one points wins the game.

Now Jill was so skilled at tossing the ball through the hoop and I was so inept that she offered me an ice cream sundae at *Dairy Queen* should I ever win a game. She was desperate for some competition.

For a week I spent every spare minute on Jill's driveway setting shots. I definitely wanted that ice-cream sundae.

"Put more arc on your throw," advised Jill. I pushed the ball higher and immediately saw improvement. Some of my shots even *swhooshed*, dropping into the net without touching the wire hoop.

"Okay, that's all the hints I'm giving you," Jill vowed.

For weeks Jill won every game. I simply didn't know how to get the one-pointers to win the ball from Jill's control, so there was no chance to try my high arching free throws.

"Use the backboard," suggested Jill.

I tried, but rather than landing in the net, my ball always rebounded out of the court.

"Roll the ball off your fingertips," she instructed.

It worked. Our games were getting closer, 21 to 15 even.

Then one fine day after accumulated hours of concentrated practice at the expense of housework and yard work, the score was 20 to 17 for Jill. I had the ball at the free-throw line. Then the remarkable happened. I looped the ball up and through the hoop, not just once, but twice to win the game.

I whooped and hollered. My jubilation literally lasted for days. I told everyone about my win whether they were interested or not. The crowning glory, the sundae, was good too. It was vanilla ice cream covered in chocolate fudge sauce and sprinkled with nuts.

> *Everyone who competes in the games goes into strict training. They do it to get a crown that will not last; but we do it to get a crown that will last forever.* (I Corinthians 9:25)

Now it seems to me if I could direct that sort of passionate behaviour to things above—and I mean higher than a basketball net—I might win souls for Christ. If I live and breathe the gospel; if I implement the lessons learned at church, and if I pray sincerely and study the Bible diligently; the Lord could surely use me beyond my wildest expectations. And the crown would be more delicious than any ice cream sundae imaginable.

I Love You, Dad

"Oh, Marian—it's you. I was going to call you."

Mom answered the phone like a kid caught with a hand in the cookie jar.

"Dad's in the hospital," she blurted.

My dad in the hospital? I couldn't believe that. He rarely came down with anything more serious than a cold.

"He's in for tests. His blood count is very low. It could be anything. Of course you try not to think the worst."

Mom had been putting off calling my brothers and me until the test results came back—no use letting us worry.

By the end of the week we knew the worst. Dad had cancer; it was in his intestines. The doctors planned to operate on the following Tuesday.

I never prayed so much for my dad in all my life. My whole church prayed for my dad. That's when I realized how much I respected and loved him and how little I had let him know.

What if he died and I didn't get a chance to thank him for my childhood? How do I say thank you for discipline I didn't want at the time? Thank you, Dad, for curbing my mouthy attitude, and thank you for refusing to let me go to the dance hall with my friends even though I acted as though you were totally unreasonable.

Thank you, Dad, for childhood Sunday walks in the woods and for knowing all about trilliums and jacks-in-the-pulpit and poison ivy and skunk cabbage.

Thank you for taking the family to the library every week and for reading.

Thanks for loving Mom so much.

And thanks for telling me that a person can pray all the time even while he or she is working. Thanks for always going to church and for not working on Sundays.

I've never met anyone with more plain common sense than my dad. He's a good listener and he knows about things. He especially knows about plants and about people. But if you ever want some advice from him you'll have to ask, because he seldom just gives it. He's smart that way.

Well, my 70-year-old dad, who has rarely been sick a day in his life, came through the operation very well. The surgeon cut out a piece of his intestines and stitched the ends back together. He told Dad that he is pretty sure he got rid of all the cancer—an assurance confirmed at Dad's most recent check-up.

A week after the operation Dad was once again watering the flowers in his greenhouse. He felt stronger each day, although he had to take a rest every afternoon.

I don't ever want to go back to assuming that my dad or my mom will always be here, because I've been confronted with the truth. They won't.

Dad, I would have a difficult time telling you face-to-face how much I love you. For fear of getting too emotional, I would leave most of it unsaid. I know you are reading this, so thanks, Dad.

> *"Honour your father and mother"—which is the first commandment with promise—"that it may go well with you and that you may enjoy long life on the earth." (Ephesians 6:2–3)*

This commandment is too good—God gives me a totally honourable father and then tells me to honour him. He promises if I do, things will go well with me, allowing me a long enjoyable life. The picture gets better. My heavenly Father is perfect and He outshines my earthly dad by light-years.

Heavenly Father, "I Love You."

The Reluctant Fisher-Woman

Together Marty and I knew as much about fishing as the average Canadian knows about the Bible. Nevertheless, we agreed to take our twelve-year-old son on a fishing holiday.

As each of our children reached the age of twelve, we have taken that child on a short vacation. We took Angela to visit her Uncle Doug in New York City. With Allison we went camping in the Allegheny Mountains.

Now Paul, who had won a tackle box at a Cadet camp-out and who had received a fishing pole from his sister for his twelfth birthday, wanted to go fishing. It was a reasonable request.

So I picked up garage-sale fishing poles at a dollar each for Marty and myself. Leaving Paul's four sisters with their grandparents, we three headed toward Balsam Lake, a lake rumoured to be alive with bass and pickerel. On our way we purchased fishing licences and plenty of groceries just in case we didn't catch dinner.

As we set up camp we acknowledged the definite fishing weather—it was raining. When the rain let up that first evening we took our poles, tackle, and Styrofoam cup full of worms to a nearby dock.

Paul tied a brightly coloured lure to his line. The salesman in the sporting goods store had said this particular lure was good for shallow water.

For myself, I chose the smallest hook I could find, reasoning that such a tiny hook would be overlooked by the fish. I wasn't too keen on dealing with live fish.

121

Handling live worms was difficult enough. The worms were fat and juicy and long—much too long for my little hook. And since I was too proud to ask Marty for help, I would have to pull one of those worms apart. I stretched the poor tortured thing out using my fingers. I finally looked away and pinched hard. Then I squeezed that little bit of worm up around my hook and dropped my line into the water.

Within two minutes I felt a tug. Since my garage-sale pole didn't include a reel, I pulled the line up hand-over-hand. I had hooked a little silvery fish no more than five inches in length. I tried to unhook it but that slippery little fish had swallowed my entire tiny hook.

Marty came to my rescue. By the time he wiggled the hook free, my poor fish had died. Marty looked at it and tossed it back in the water. "It's much too small," he said.

During the next twenty minutes I caught four more tiny fish. Each time I felt a nibble I would silently hope the fish would go away. It didn't. I kept several fish in a pail for awhile, but Marty insisted we throw my entire catch back. "A person could get arrested for keeping baby fish," he cautioned. Marty caught one fish even smaller than mine and Paul hooked a big one, but it got away.

Paul appreciated his weekend, "I liked being with you guys." And we all know more about fishing now.

> "Come, follow me," Jesus said, "and I will make you fishers of men." (Matthew 4:19)

I approach both kinds of fishing with the same reluctance. I put a little hook out here or there—hoping I won't get a bite. Then when I get a bite, I don't attempt follow-up. If I look closely at what Jesus actually said, I can be encouraged. He doesn't say, "Be fishers of men." He says, "Come, follow me, and I (Jesus) will make you fishers of men." The secret to successful evangelism is to have a relationship with Jesus.

How Does One Deal With Death? With Life?

At 74, Marty's dad appeared to be an active, healthy man with nothing so seriously wrong with him that a hearing aid couldn't fix. We assumed he would be around at least another twenty years: feeding his steers, planting his garden, driving sick old-people to doctor's appointments, writing letters to the editor, hooking rugs, playing with his grandchildren, and doing the 800 other things that kept him busy from morning until nightfall.

Then suddenly this past summer he complained about a backache. Even with rest the backache persisted. There were blood tests which led to more tests which pinpointed the problem: cancer of the pancreas with lesions on the liver.

He spent his last two weeks on earth tidying up his financial affairs (not that they were ever messy), arranging funeral details, and saying good-bye to family, friends and neighbours. He died at home one evening shortly after family devotions at his bedside. That was the day he lost his ability to swallow. He died at peace with the full assurance that soon he would have a new body. Days earlier he had mentioned, with a twinkle in his eye, that he was looking forward to having his hearing restored.

At the funeral there was an underlying joy mingled with the sorrow of missing a loved one. We knew he was in heaven with Jesus. As the minister put it, "He's gone ahead." And as our twelve-year-old son said, "I can look forward to seeing Opa in about 80 years."

After the funeral, back at the homestead while eating salads and casseroles prepared by loving members of the church, I sat beside Carol, a non-Christian friend of Marty's missionary sister. "Must be quite a shock to your kids to suddenly lose their grandfather," she commented.

I looked at her, briefly wondering if I should talk to her honestly, as if she were a Christian, as if she would understand. I decided to go ahead.

"Actually, they're pretty good with it," I said, picturing my five children. "There's been tears and they'll miss him, but you know, he said good-bye to each one of them and told them to live for the Lord. They'll always remember that. That's special...and," I added, "they know he's in heaven."

She looked at me curiously, "Is everyone in the family so strongly religious?"

That left me tongue-tied. Obviously she saw all the faith and assurance stuff as a made-up, organized set of beliefs. I had wanted to give her the truth, serve it to her like a piece of cake, but alas, I didn't even know how to cut into the cake. As Christians we know death is a step along the road into eternity, but that was only so much mumbo-jumbo to Carol.

Our conversation left me with a couple of questions. How does someone, who thinks this life is everything, deal with death? How does that person deal with life? Or, if someone doesn't believe in Jesus, but suspects there could possibly be something beyond the reaches of this life, how does he or she dare approach death?

> *My message and my preaching were not with wise and persuasive words, but with a demonstration of the Spirit's power, so that your faith might not rest on men's wisdom, but on God's power. (1 Corinthians 2:4–5)*

As I re-examine my conversation with Carol and reconsider my questions about life and death, I realize the Holy Spirit knows all the answers. To be an effective witness, I need *God's power*.

Genetic Tears

I would not obey my teachers or listen to my instructors. (Proverb 5:13)

"My teacher is very patient," reported four-year-old Amanda after several weeks of junior kindergarten at the local public school. I should have realized there was more behind her statement.

That Friday while I stood at the classroom door among several other parents waiting to walk our children home, the teacher singled me out, "Amanda's Mom, we didn't have such a good day today," she said. "You and I had better talk." She arranged to have me come to see her when the children would be with the gymnasium instructor the following Monday.

This was a first. Not one of Amanda's four older siblings in a combined 32 years of schooling had ever behaved in a way which required a talk with their teacher. Over the years there had been minor problems, but I hadn't been summoned by a teacher since my own school days.

On the way across the playing field towards our home Amanda suggested, "My teacher is not so patient anymore."

"So what happened?" I asked casually.

"I don't have to play when she wants me to!" Amanda looked at me with her big determined brown eyes.

"Yes, you do," I countered.

She continued, "I don't have to pick a book when she wants me to."

"Yes you do," I repeated. "You should obey God, your parents and your teacher. The only time you don't have to listen to your teacher is if she tells you to do something bad—and I don't think Mrs. Van Sickle would do that!" I stated emphatically.

After some tears, Amanda said she would obey. I knew she meant it when several hours later I found her in the family room dancing in a circle, chanting, "I will obey God, I will obey God and my mom and my dad and my teacher."

That Sunday in church a providential children's message about obeying God, your parents, your baby sitter and your teacher reinforced my instruction.

On Monday morning I entered Amanda's classroom prepared to tell the teacher about Amanda's resolve to obey. I watched as the children went through their opening exercises including a jazzed up rendition of "O Canada."

After the teacher dismissed the children to the gym, she led me to a little table and invited me to sit on a tiny chair. From her own little perch on the other side of the table, she looked at me, "Is there something going on at home that we should know about?"

I wasn't prepared for this question. "No, I don't think so," I muttered. Couldn't she see Amanda was from a warm and caring, Christian family? Apparently not.

The teacher continued, "She was running down the hall to the library and I said, 'No Amanda' and right away there were the tears."

Was that it? I assured the teacher that the quick-flowing tears were genetic. Some den Boers simply don't like to be told they are doing something wrong. It makes them cry.

"Ignore the tears," I advised.

She did.

Amanda has been obeying her ever since.

> *He who scorns instruction will pay for it, but he who respects a command is rewarded. (Proverbs 13:13)*

Years after this incident, 15-year-old Amanda set me straight. Her tears had been tears of pain and frustration. Her stomach hurt. The teacher had told her to hurry and then, not to run.

Even though the teacher, Amanda, and I, each had a different slightly skewed view of what was happening, through it all, Amanda learned a valuable lesson about obedience.

Secrets of a Driving Instructor

"How do you pick things to write about?" my brother-in-law asked.

"There are lots of things I'd like to write about, but don't," I replied.

"Like...?"

"Like things Angela does. She'd never give me permission."

Angela's eyes opened wide. "Like what?" she challenged.

"Like, I'm taking you out driving tomorrow. I probably won't be able to write about that," I stated.

Angela, her newly acquired beginner's permit burning in her pocket, had driven in a parking lot once with her father. He came back shaking his head and she came back begging that I go with her next time. "He expects me to know everything already," she lamented.

Angela had also driven the family van the final mile to Oma den Boer's house in the country where we were spending a few days during Christmas holidays. That little trip with Angela at the wheel produced large butterflies in my stomach. I think it was because she tended to drive on the very edge of the road, very near the ditch.

Just thinking about our upcoming lesson knotted my insides. I prayed, "Lord keep us safe and help me be a good teacher."

I remembered Mr. Tripp, my high school defensive driving instructor who went out with entire classes of teenagers, three at a time. He exuded calmness. He always sat back, casually sucking mints. He never raised his voice.

We saw him as a man who enjoyed his job and did it well.

And why not? Even though he was at least 50, he could spend several hours each day cruising the countryside with bright and witty 16-year-olds and get paid for it.

The driving lesson

That Boxing Day morning when Angela and I headed out on her driving lesson, there was practically no traffic on the country road where Oma lived. The lack of traffic made it somewhat easier for me to exude a Mr. Tripp-like calmness.

At one point, a large farm vehicle approached. I don't recall just what it was—I was too busy thinking about slipping into the roadside gully as Angela steered wide of the approaching vehicle.

Our next test was a German shepherd trotting towards us on the right shoulder of the road as we made our way up a hill and around a corner. Angela gasped and veered blindly across to the left side of the road. Thankfully there was no oncoming traffic.

"Umm, Angela, the life of that dog is not as valuable as ours," I quietly hinted.

The dog episode was followed by several challenge-free minutes. Angela looked over at me and smiled, "See, I haven't given you anything to write about." As she gazed at me waiting for an answer, the van drifted across the road.

"Uuhh..." I uttered quietly pointing ahead.

"Whoops."

I continued to direct Angela up and down numerous side roads and in our effort to avoid major highways, she turned around in countless farm lanes. Her skills improved as the minutes ticked by.

"Why do you keep looking at your watch?" she asked. "Is this boring for you?"

"Oh, no," I assured her. To maintain my Mr. Tripp veneer I thought it best to not mention the turmoil in my digestive system. It occurred to me, those mints Mr. Tripp was always popping—they must have been Tums.

The Lord did answer my prayer. After an hour we arrived back at the house unscathed, and I'm sure not even Mr. Tripp could have done a better teaching job.

But when he, the Spirit of truth, comes, he will guide you into all truth. (John 16:13)

As we drive the road of life the Holy Spirit is our teacher. Unobtrusively directing us, guiding us, loving us, and letting us learn from our mistakes, He's the ultimate teacher. He doesn't make mistakes and doesn't need Tums as he guides us *into all truth.*

Now that My Husband is My Boss...

Marty has generally been a kind, romantic, loyal and loving husband. According to one of his former secretaries, Marty was also a considerate and understanding boss. Thus this past fall when he started up his own accounting firm, I applied to be Marty's secretary.

He hesitated to hire me. As an accountant he wanted things done accurately and precisely. He figured I might be a bit too "creative." He knew consistency bored me, but I assured him I was willing to curb my inventive instincts. I told him I would follow set procedures. The possibility of some other woman at my husband's beck and call in our basement home office might have contributed to my rash promises.

When Marty agreed to hire me, it became my job to do the sort of things I had made a point of *not* doing throughout our marriage. In keeping with my personal philosophy I never polished Marty's shoes or packed his suitcase. My philosophy was based on the premise, "give him an inch and he'll take a mile." I might end up cutting his nails and brushing his teeth.

But as Marty's secretary I naturally acquired all the menial work. I had to order things for him, set up appointments, type letters, buy stamps, stuff envelopes, etc.

Working for my husband was certainly not like being his wife. Our marriage was a partnership. We would give and take. We discussed and there was always room for innovation.

In the office he was the boss. That was okay—except I didn't take orders very well. Those first few months were a lesson in servanthood.

Our conversations at various levels of irritation included phrases such as:

Marty: The mailing is all wrong.
Myself: Whoops, I didn't see those return envelopes.

Marty: And where's the letter I told you to set aside?
Myself: On your desk, SIR.

Myself: I've never had a boss who expected me to know things right away.
Marty: I've never had a secretary who didn't know things.

When I prepared a mailing incorrectly, I tore open the envelopes and re-stuffed them, all the while grumbling at Marty for getting so upset about a simple little mistake. I actually stomped out of the office once, threatening to find another job where my employer would understand and appreciate me.

To our credit, our squabbles never lasted beyond the immediate situation and we always kissed and made up according to the, "don't let the sun go down on your anger principle."

As time passed the fights became fewer. Now five months into the venture, I am reasonably content. My personal philosophy is even changing. What's wrong with doing the servant things? As Jesus said to his disciples,

> ...you also should wash one another's feet. (John 13:14b)

Some situations highlight how unlike Christ we are. When I was obligated to do the servant things for my husband/boss, I recognized my aversion to servanthood which for me was synonymous with slavery. During my five-month confinement, my motivation moved from the defensive "no one is going to take advantage of me" to the assertive "what can I do to help."

I am learning to serve.

My Pastor's Sermon Changed My Life

The end of all things is near. Therefore be clear minded and self-controlled so that you can pray. (1 Peter 4:7)

My wilful nature and a sermon by our pastor, warning members of the congregation against leaving the mainstream to look for signs at places such as the Vineyard in Toronto, sent me directly there to investigate.

I had been avoiding the "Toronto Blessing." It sounded a bit too hokey for my Calvinist mind. I had friends who were quietly inviting me, but I always had a very good reason not to go. Yet, while in church listening to a sermon that told me just what I wanted to hear, I suddenly felt defensive for my friends. How could my pastor warn against their Christian fellowship? I wanted to talk to him, but could I do this knowing nothing firsthand?

That very Sunday a friend once again invited me to spend the evening with her at the Vineyard. This time I jumped at the chance. At the Vineyard the guest preacher told us we were living in the last times between the first and second coming of the Lord and we should be striving to make this world the place the Lord intended it to be. We should be working, not just waiting. My Calvinist mind felt right at home.

Then it was ministry time. The chairs in the back half of the room were moved and hundreds of people arranged themselves side-by-side on parallel lengths of yellow tape on the floor. The strips of tape were about six feet apart and stretched a distance of at least 70 feet. My friend led me to an unoccupied stretch of tape where we stood waiting in anticipation. The first ministry team that came to pray with me prayed that my eyes and ears would be opened. I agreed in prayer. The second team prayed that I receive prophetic intercession. I agreed after I figured out "intercession" was Vineyard language for "prayer." Then I felt very hot, fell to the carpet and began laughing the most spontaneous laughing I had ever experienced.

The following week I didn't want to stop praying. I would pray all day, wake after sleeping about an hour, and pray all night as well. After a week of that you can imagine my physical condition. As Marty's secretary, I was useless.

My ability to reason became next to nil. When I set out to pick up my daughter from a youth meeting, I couldn't find the right house, so I ended up driving around all night praying for the world. It didn't actually occur to me that Marty and the kids would worry.

When I came home at 9:30 the next morning, I was surprised to see our driveway packed with cars and the living room filled with friends who had gathered to comfort Marty and pray that I would be found.

A visit to the family doctor led me to the hospital and subsequently to the psychiatric ward where the doctors interviewed me, identified my condition as manic-depressive and put me on the corresponding medication. After two weeks they sent me home with a year's prescription for lithium.

The following week a Christian psychiatrist analyzed my situation. He took me off the lithium and recommended adequate rest: he explained that sleep deprivation leads to delusions.

Basically, after a week without much sleep, I had lost touch with the concrete world.

After that, I spent my nights sleeping, and during the day I prayed—*"clear minded and self-controlled."*

> *But God chose the foolish things of the world to shame the wise; God chose the weak things of the world to shame the strong. He chose the lowly things of this*

> world and the despised things—and the things that are not—to nullify the things that are, so that no one may boast before him. (1 Corinthians 1:27–29)

Following my Holy Spirit encounter, life would never be the same. Now that my barriers and coping mechanisms were down, the Holy Spirit would be able to show me my self-righteousness. Sometimes these things are messy.

New Testimony

I had been a self-righteous, white-washed sepulchre,
until I realized Jesus, anointed with sweet-smelling myrrh,
seated at the right hand of my heavenly Father
washed me in blood, not just water.
In His righteousness I can stand
to do all He planned,
with power from on high,
yet...my old self has to die.

He opened my heart,
the Holy Spirit to impart.
He changed my life completely
(and not very neatly).
I was a baby with surgeons' tools.
I didn't know the rules.
For all the preaching,
I had no teaching.
When the spiritual realm opened wide,
I was but a babe inside.

Psalm 51 As It Happened to Me

Purify me from my sins, and I will be clean; wash me, and I will be whiter than snow. Oh give me back my joy again; you have broken me—now let me rejoice. (Psalm 51:7–8, New Living Translation)

When I asked the Lord to purify me,
The thought of pain didn't occur,
Until I couldn't sleep.
Confusing, wicked schemes
Whirled through my head all night.

Without love, joy or peace
I went to a friend's house and accused her of nonsense.
Patience, kindness and goodness escaped me.
Faithfulness, gentleness and self-control were impossible.

I went to the doctor;
He gave me pills to dull my brain.
Friends tried to comfort me.
My pastor prayed.

I went to Christian counsellors;
The Holy Spirit showed them the garbage I was carrying.
They commanded away wrong spirits
Too numerous and filthy to mention.
I went home;
I knew there wasn't a single thing I could do

That would make God say,
"That's my girl. Isn't she good!"

I questioned why He would even want my worship.
I saw all my prayers tainted with sin.
I cried—I felt so dirty.
I was broken.

Then for the first time I knew,
Really knew in my spirit—
Not just in my mind—
Jesus is my only righteousness.

My joy is coming back.

It Just Never Got Warm

The real estate listing said "gas furnace," but that was a lie. When we purchased our home, it came with a forced-air electric furnace. "An expensive way to heat the house," our agent observed.

The previous owner pointed out that a gas furnace might explode—he knew of two such incidents. He said an electric furnace was much safer. Members of his family were afraid of gas.

That first September, several months after we had purchased our home, the previous owner returned. "I thought I'd better hook up a few wires for you," he said. He led Marty and me to a shelf in the furnace room where he picked up three unconnected short blue wires. He attached them among a tangle of yellow, green and white wires at the back of the furnace. He had removed the blue wires from the furnace in the spring so that the furnace wouldn't kick in when the air-conditioner was supposed to be working. "Make sure you turn off the electricity before you try this," he warned. "You could get electrocuted."

In October when we got around to turning the furnace on, nothing happened. It didn't work. Our friend the electrician traced the problem to the thermostat in the dining room. Someone had brushed against it and loosened the connection. The furnace wasn't getting any messages.

Then it got messages. By December the furnace ran continuously most days. On very cold days the parts of the house closest to the furnace would be almost comfortable by noon. The upstairs bedrooms and the living room on the north side of the house never really got warm.

On very cold days we took to lighting and opening the gas oven in the kitchen during breakfast. It was either that or wear gloves at the table.

By spring the heating bill totalled $1500. That was when Marty, the accountant, looked into replacing the furnace.

The fellow who installed the shiny new gas furnace showed us the workings of the old electric furnace. Inside it looked like a giant toaster. The toaster had a fan which was supposed to gently blow the toasted air up the vents throughout the house.

Our new gas furnace took up less space than the giant toaster and could heat the whole house in half an hour for a third of the cost. Now, let the cold winter come—we've got a fire in our furnace.

Our electric furnace could be compared to the Old Testament covenant of the law with its rules and regulations. Thankfully just like our electric furnace that covenant has been replaced.

> *But now, by dying to what once bound us, we have been released from the law so that we serve in the new way of the Spirit, and not in the old way of the written code. (Romans 7:6)*

"Lord, show me how to live by the Spirit instead of merely being guided by dos and don'ts. You've given me a new covenant; I want to live by it."

The Parable of
the Pool

When we purchased our present home last summer, it came with a somewhat neglected in-ground pool. In an effort to care for this pool I visited pool shops, attended pool school and read *The Pool Book* from cover to cover. I became obsessed with achieving the sparkling clean water the pool people talked about. There was a picture of this water in *The Pool Book*.

Yet, somehow our water was less than sparkling when we closed the pool in the fall during a drizzling rain. All winter I wondered what was happening beneath that grey cover. We'd thrown in the suggested chemicals but was that enough?

In the spring when we removed the winter cover, Marty was ready to rent a back-hoe and fill in the whole thing. The pool liner had pulled away at the top edges and was drooping all along one side. The pool bottom was covered with a layer of black silt. The water was murky green.

Two days later, after suctioning water from behind the liner and spending hours kneeling along the pool edge pouring boiling water on the liner to make it pliable and then tucking this more workable liner back into its groove, Marty and I examined our raw knuckles and knees. Was a pool worth this?

I vacuumed the bottom only to see clouds of black grime come shooting back into the pool through the side return jet. This problem led to repeated vacuuming and—eventually after much troubleshooting—to the purchase of a new filter. As for the murkiness, according to the pool shop and other pool owners, we needed a combination of baking soda, chlorine and stabilizer. The pool shop sold liquid chlorine from a tap. Rather than buy a new container (I am Dutch, after all) I dragged out a large blue plastic barrel I had used to make beer, some 20 years earlier.

In the driveway at home as I unloaded the chlorine from the back of the van, the old beer barrel cracked.

I bounced the cracked container onto its side on the front lawn and watched at least ten dollars soak into the lawn where to this day there is still a brown patch. I decided to put the remaining chlorine into a pail. But first I exchanged my good clothes for baggy white shorts and an old shirt.

I should have worn shoes. Have you ever stepped into a puddle of chlorine? Don't. It burns. There I was on the front lawn dancing to and fro on my burning feet while balancing a broken barrel half full of chlorine over a pail, and then my baggy white shorts started to slip down. Rather than splash chlorine over myself, I let them go.

Then I laughed. I laughed because this reminded me of spiritual warfare. I should have put on the belt of truth and the shoes of readiness in the gospel. I shouldn't have used an old wineskin. And there is only one source of truly sparkling clean water: Jesus Christ.

> *You were taught with regard to your former way of life, to put off your old self, which is being corrupted by its deceitful desires; to be made new in the attitude of your minds; and to put on the new self, created to be like God in true righteousness and holiness. (Ephesians 4:22–24)*

The Holy Spirit has been revealing the murky depths of my old self and making me new in the attitude of my mind. He points me to Jesus Christ the sparkling clean water and source of true righteousness and holiness. He calls for my prayerful co-operation and leads me to put on the full armour of God so that I can take my stand against the devil's schemes (See Ephesians 6).

The Automatic Garage-Door Opener

Right now our automatic garage-door opener is not connected to our big double garage door. After the accident, we haven't been able to get the door quite lined up with its track.

The accident is something we don't talk about much. You see, it wasn't impulsive, day-dreaming me who backed into the garage door; it was careful, with-it, in-control Marty. He's still wondering how this happened.

Unfamiliarity—that might explain something about the accident. Before we moved to this place we never owned a garage big enough to hold our car. For us the automatic garage-door opener was a new gadget—something to learn about.

Also, on the day of the accident Marty had been working hard at his desk from early morning right into the evening. So, when intent on running a few errands, he stepped into the van parked inside the closed garage, he may not have been as sharp as usual. Fourteen hours of looking at numbers can do that to a person.

Marty slid into the driver's seat, pushed the remote control garage-door opener, turned the key in the ignition and backed up. "Bang!" The garage door didn't have a chance. It wasn't more than a foot up when Marty turned around to see what the noise could possibly be. He had dented the door, knocking it right off its rails. The van was fine.

Marty spent an entire Saturday with the help of a friend disassembling, banging, straightening and reassembling the garage door. They restored the door to open manually, but they couldn't line it up precisely enough to engage the sensitive automatic opener.

For the rest of the summer we parked our vehicles out on the driveway and used the garage door as little as possible. It opened fine manually, but the extra effort didn't seem worthwhile. The cold harsh winter motivated us to make the extra effort. And now that we have experienced the ease of an automatic garage door opener, we have resolved to get ourselves a new garage door that will line up perfectly with the tracks.

> *I thank God that I speak in tongues more than all of you. (I Corinthians 14:18)*

Our garage door experience makes me think of prayer. Praying "manually" or with the mind works, but praying in tongues is like having an automatic garage-door opener—I open my mouth and let the Spirit control my tongue. The Holy Spirit knows exactly how to pray about every situation. My part is simply to line up with Him in love. If I don't have love, when I pray I am merely "a resounding gong or a clanging symbol" as mentioned in 1 Corinthians 13:1.

A Storm in the Living Room

According to the neighbours, the man who built our present home for himself ten years ago was not a builder but a pastor. I thought that might explain why it rained inside our living room during Hurricane Opal. Then again, you can't blame everything on the pastor.

When we bought the house we knew there was a problem with the roof above the front section of the living room which protrudes about six feet out from beneath the master bedroom. We knew because there were watermarks and lumpy patches on the living room ceiling.

One of the first things Marty did after we bought the house was climb up on that part of the roof and caulk around the flashing and other places water might seep in. After that we hired a plasterer to patch the living room ceiling properly. He did a fine job matching the design perfectly.

Then came the tail of Hurricane Opal with her driving, torrential rains. During the height of the storm, Marty heard a "plink" in the living room where he discovered a small puddle growing on our coffee table. We pushed the furniture back, and placed a large plastic pail where the coffee table had been.

Plunk, plunk, plunk; a new drip started over by the couch. This was quickly followed by several others across the width of the room in line with the outside wall of our upstairs bedroom. We placed pails, bowls and pans as each successive drip emerged. Soon we had an array of pots, pans and pails filling steadily. We emptied the containers and set them out again just before retiring for the night.

In the morning the storm was over outside, but we could still hear the occasional drip in our living room. The large plastic pail had filled to within an inch of spilling over. The other pails, pots and pans were at various levels of full, and several contained large hunks of plaster. Our ceiling was a mess.

A few weeks later we had a roofer/renovator in to analyze our problem. He came down from the roof scratching his head. "Everything looks watertight and properly done. Can't see where the rain would get in." He paused, "Unless it got absorbed in through the brick wall. That looks like a rather porous brick." He suggested we seal it on a dry summer day.

> *For if you live according to the sinful nature, you will die; but if by the Spirit you put to death the misdeeds of the body, you will live, because those who are led by the Spirit of God are sons of God.(Romans 8:13–14)*

Like the outside wall of our upstairs bedroom, my personal philosophy was built with porous brick. I had given my life, but not all of it, to Jesus. The devil could have that part of me that was bound to sin. For, I reasoned, nobody could be perfect and this was me. Like the porous brick, my philosophy was full of holes. By not committing my whole being to Jesus, I put myself in a state of death. I must put to death the misdeeds of the body, not hang on to sinful behaviour buttressed with excuses.

Out of Love for My Husband

Since the kitchen was mostly my domain, I made the decision to paint the door frames of the sliding glass door a bright aqua-turquoise. I did this without consulting Marty who is, after all, less imaginative than myself. Even he would have to agree that anything was better than the existing dull grey metal.

When he showed some concern about my colour choice, I assured him I had an overall strategy. "Don't worry, Honey, I know what I'm doing," I said, knowing he would fall in love with the idea once he saw the finished door. Less creative types have a hard time visualizing.

Several days and three coats of paint later, Marty told me as gently as a husband can that I had made a mistake.

"Oh, you'll get used to it," I said brightly. "I'm making ruffled curtains to match for the window by the sink."

When the curtains were hung Marty remained unconvinced. I wasn't defeated though. I began soliciting honest opinions. Our children were noncommittal, or disinterested, or just plain wise to stay out of the discussion. My mother thought the colour was tacky. My father considered it creative, but Marty's mom really didn't like it. Our friends mostly waltzed around the subject, seeing this as a family issue.

The colour choice hadn't worked out quite the way I expected. As the months passed, rather than Marty warming up to the aqua-turquoise on the door frames, I was beginning to question my own good judgment. Was it tacky? Would the room look better if the door frames were blue or boring brown or even harvest gold to match my trusty old stove and dishwasher?

Marty finally suggested painting the door frames a pale yellow to match the walls. By then, I was at least ready to admit that he disliked the aqua-turquoise more than I liked it. So, you might say out of love for my husband I repainted the door frames a pale yellow.

This time the work took even longer than the first time. Painting a light colour over a bright colour is rather a tedious business, especially when it's not your own idea.

After two coats, Marty examined my work. "Guess it needs a third coat, eh?" was the advice he offered. I knew that; I could see the bits of aqua-turquoise poking through. Still, it made me angry for him to say it.

Yet, once that third coat was on, I had to admit the pale yellow looked great.

> *This then is how you should pray: "Our Father in heaven, hallowed be your name, your kingdom come, your will be done on earth as it is in heaven." (Matthew 6;9–10)*

The relationship between Christ and His Church can be a lot like this husband/wife thing. We, the Church, sometimes insist on doing things our own way. After all, we are the Church. We know how to worship, how to run programs, how to evangelize. Of course the Lord will approve our decisions. After all, He gave us these responsibilities.

But Christ patiently waits for His bride to come around.

She Loves Me

Out of the blue, Pat phoned: would I mind taking care of little Suzy, her poodle, for a couple of days? I thought maybe Pat had dialled the wrong number. I dislike pets. Ask my kids. Animals belong in a barn, and I'm glad I'm not a farmer.

Anyway I agreed to take Suzy so Pat could go to a Vineyard conference on the love of God. I'm a soft touch when it comes to Christian fellowship. And my children like pets.

The next day Suzy, the poodle, arrived with all her paraphernalia.

"She likes what we eat—spaghetti, weenies." Pat produced a bag with several cans inside.

"She goes to bed about 11 o'clock." Pat handed me a basket filled with a big fluffy pillow.

"She wears this sweater outside when it's cold." Pat held up a little red sweater.

"She's a woman's dog." Pat looked at me.

Suzy was about the size, if not the shape, of a football. Amanda and Michelle loved her immediately. They wanted to play with her, but that little grey yapping bundle of curly fur ignored them.

"Here, throw her tiger and see what she does," I said, tossing Suzy's stuffed tiger down the hallway. She ran after it and held the tiger in her mouth, daring me to take it from her. Every time I approached, she dodged out of my reach until she was ready to let me grab the thing.

"She wants to play keep-away," I instructed the girls. I gave the tiger to Michelle. She tossed it. Suzy sat down, turned her head and looked the other way. The game was over.

Suzy followed me around. She cried at the door when I left to do errands. When she had to go outside, I was the only one who could put her sweater on. For me, disdainer of pets, all this affection from a dog was somewhat overwhelming.

As bedtime approached, we humans decided Suzy should sleep in her basket in Amanda's room. She was probably used to sleeping close to people, we reasoned.

At 11 p.m. I lead Suzy into Amanda's room. Amanda was fast asleep. Suzy jumped onto the bed and curled up. Wondering what the basket was for, I tip-toed off to my place beside Marty in the master bedroom.

Five minutes later Suzy was scratching and yipping at the master bedroom door. I opened the door. She ran in and jumped up on the bed where she eventually settled on top of the blankets between Marty and me in the crook behind my knees. I had a pretty good night except I woke up every time I tried to roll over.

When Pat came back to pick up Suzy, I exclaimed, "She loves me."

I hadn't done anything to earn her love. She just loved me.

And I pray that you, being rooted and established in love, may...grasp how wide and long and high and deep is the love of Christ...(Ephesians 3:17b–18)

Suzy's love and attention was no doubt a learned behaviour. She knew the benefit of being cosy with the woman of the house. She could kiss the hand that feeds her.

God's love is immeasurably wider, longer, higher and deeper. He went to the depths of the cross and hell. Christ rose to the height of interceding for us at the right hand of our heavenly Father. The width and length of His love is eternal. That is pure undeserved, unearned, unadulterated love. I want to be rooted and established in that love.

Losing My Licence

One sunny winter day Michelle and I put on several layers of shirts and sweaters so we wouldn't need bulky coats. I tucked my driver's licence into my breast pocket so I wouldn't need a purse. We loaded the cross-country skis into the van and we were off to the local golf course. Apart from a few spills we had a wonderful afternoon.

It wasn't until Sunday morning two days later that I realized my licence wasn't in my purse. I quickly checked my shirt pocket. It wasn't there either. Panic set in. I must have lost the licence on the golf course. It could have slipped out when I failed to negotiate a turn and landed in the weeds.

Maybe I could check the course. Or maybe someone would find the licence and mail it to me. Maybe I could go to the licence bureau on Monday and arrange for a new one. In the meantime, did that mean I shouldn't drive?

Coincidentally, that Sunday morning some friends whose car was giving them trouble needed our help to get to church. Their car lost power whenever it faced a major challenge like a hill. They didn't have power to drive their vehicle and I didn't have the authority to drive ours.

Sitting in church I wondered if I really had lost the authority to drive a car just because I misplaced the piece of paper that proved my authority. It wasn't the same as the time years ago when Marty lost his licence because he hadn't paid a speeding ticket. I mean, I still legally had my licence. I just didn't know where the proof was. Of course, with all this going through my mind I missed part of the service.

Sunday afternoon conditions were still ideal for skiing, so Marty and I and two of our children decided to return to the golf course. We would keep our eyes open for my licence along the trail.

As we dressed for skiing I grabbed a flannel shirt. There in the breast pocket was the licence. That's what can happen when you wear layers of shirts.

> *I tell you the truth, anyone who has faith in me will do what I have been doing. He will do even greater things than these, because I am going to the Father. (John 14:12)*

This is our licence. Too often, we in the church think we don't have the licence to do what Jesus teaches in the gospels; while all along, proof of our authority is right there in Scripture. When we recognize the authority we have through Christ's resurrection, the power of the Holy Spirit is able to work through us.

The Culprit

I'd like to blame my whole ordeal on Marty's zippy little car. Surely I wouldn't have been zooming down a city street at 79 klicks per hour if I'd been behind the wheel of the family van.

I was driving along joyfully singing praises to the Lord on my way to pick up Angela and Allison from school on the first real spring afternoon of the season. Suddenly I noticed a white car with a blue and white stripe and a flashing red light, coming out of a side street up ahead. This car appeared to be in a great hurry. I quickly slowed down to give it the right of way.

The police officer inside the car under the flashing red light had another plan. He pointed directly at me and motioned that I pull over to the curb.

My song stopped. My heart sank. I did as he directed. There I was, parked at the side of the street on a gorgeous spring afternoon with my window rolled down and a lump in my stomach.

The officer walked up alongside, "How are you?"

"Feelin' kinda sad," I replied.

He nodded.

"People are driving faster along here than on Highway 6. We've had complaints. May I see your driver's licence?"

I took my wallet out of the purse beside me and pulled out the licence. I handed it to him.

"And your insurance?"

That was more difficult to locate. I extracted a little crumpled pink paper marked 1993. "That's not it. It's in here somewhere," I mumbled as I shuffled through the stack of cards and papers I'd been carrying around inside my wallet. "1992, 1994."

"You wonder why people keep those?" the policeman mused.

I could have told him about never having time to find the old insurance card when my husband handed me the new one. Or, I could have mentioned my secret fear of throwing out the wrong insurance card, but I kept my mouth shut. The poor, little, sad, puppy routine usually got me further than any amount of yapping. I was hoping for the police officer's pity and maybe just a warning.

The policeman waved my licence, "I'll go check this out. You keep looking."

By the time he returned, I had the up-to-date insurance card and he had a freshly written ticket for me.

"I adjusted the charge down to 70 in a 50," he said kindly.

"What's that in money?" I wanted to know.

"They don't make it cheap for you nowadays. It's $80 for speeding and a $15 surcharge."

I thanked him and dropped the ticket onto the seat beside me. I waited for him to get back into his cruiser before I eased onto the road where I poked along at an exact 50 kilometres per hour. I still made it to the school in plenty of time to pick up the girls. While waiting for them I studied the ticket. The $15 charge was a "victim" surcharge. Did that mean I was a victim? I thought I was the culprit. I certainly qualified for the ticket. Maybe I was the victim of the surcharge. I wondered what would happen if I didn't pay that part of the ticket.

> *He (Jesus) said to them (the Pharisees), "You are the ones who justify yourselves in the eyes of men, but God knows your hearts. What is highly valued among men is detestable in God's sight." (Luke 16:15)*

My speeding along city streets praising the Lord is a picture of what Jesus is talking about to the Pharisees. It was a lovely spring day, I had a zippy little car and a song in my heart—isn't that enough justification for speeding? And why did I have to pay such a huge fine?

God wants us to do things the way He reveals in His Word. We want to adjust things to suit our whims. That is not acceptable. In fact Jesus said people who break commandments and teach others to do so *will be called least in the kingdom of heaven. (Matthew 5:19)*

When am I going to make Jesus the Lord of my whole life?

Cleaning Up

One gusty, grey, garbage-day morning while waiting patiently in the van in the driveway for Angela and Allison so I could drive them to school, I noticed some of the garbage from the townhouses across the road had blown into the middle of the intersection next to our home.

I had an urge to run out and pick up this garbage, but I noticed a garbage man in a reflector vest pacing on the other side of the road apparently waiting for traffic to subside so he could do it.

Then I realized he didn't intend to pick up the garbage; he was merely watching it. Now why would that be? Maybe the garbage people were fed up with the way garbage was always allowed to blow around. Maybe this was evidence for a supervisor to behold.

On the drive to the girls' school and home again, I pondered the garbage situation. I came to the conclusion that the only neighbourly thing to do would be to pick up that garbage myself.

Sure enough when I came back to the intersection, the garbage was still in the middle of the road, but now a garbage truck was parked right beside it—and not a garbage man in sight. There was hardly room for my vehicle to drive by.

I parked the van, then marched into the intersection where I picked up a Tide box and a much larger box. For boxes that had blown out onto the road, they were surprisingly heavy. In fact, I noticed they were packed with garbage, but I doggedly carried them to the sidewalk.

"Ma'am, ma'am. What are you doing?" I heard as I heaved the Tide box onto the garbage pile in front of the townhouses where I was sure it had come from. I was about to drag the larger box over as well.

"I'm cleaning up," I proclaimed indignantly. "There is no reason to keep garbage in the middle of the road."

"Yes, there is, ma'am," he explained patiently. "We spilled hydraulic fluid here. Our line sprang a leak. If a car drives over that it could cause a serious accident."

"Oh sorry," I mumbled as I dropped the big heavy makeshift pylon back onto the road. For the first time I noticed the slippery oily fluid all over my hands.

When I got home I had to scrub my hands and wash both my coat and pants.

Moral of the story: don't be too quick to judge other people's garbage.

> *How can you say to your brother, 'Let me take the speck out of your eye,' when all the time there is a plank in your own eye? (Matthew 7:4)*

How often do we as good Christian citizens judge and try to clean up someone else's garbage? What we judge as garbage may really be pylons. Wouldn't it be better to come alongside? Be a friend. Listen. Find out what's really needed. Offer to be available. That way we're less likely to end up with oily goo all over ourselves.

The Lightning of God

Even though I was studying a book that referred to intercessory prayer as "The Lightning of God," I never really thought of the prayers we send up on behalf of others as lightning, that is, until lightning struck our house.

All seven of us were comfortably in our respective beds one 5 a.m. when a particularly loud clap of thunder woke most of the family and caused Marty to comment, "That was close!" We rolled over and went back to sleep.

In the morning Amanda got up first. She came running to the bedrooms with a piece of brick she had found on the floor by the fireplace. Angela was the one to realize our chimney had been struck by lightning. Marty and I quickly dressed and exited our second-storey bedroom through the window onto the roof to get a look. Sure enough, the entire top of the chimney had been knocked clear off. Pieces of brick were scattered below among smashed patio furniture.

As the day progressed we realized the garage-door opener had shorted out, the fax/phone wasn't working properly and the computer had a problem.

Lightning can rearrange and change things. So can prayer. Just ask Amanda. Several months after the lightning incident, she added a line to her prayers that went something like this, "Lord, please give us a little baby in our family."

I asked her politely, "Please don't say that prayer." At her next prayer time she prayed quietly. When she finally opened her eyes and unfolded her hands she smiled happily, "I prayed for a baby again." This continued for more than a week.

Well, we are going to have a baby much to the surprise of everyone except Amanda, who, when she heard the announcement, exclaimed, "And I did it all by myself!"

"No, God did it," Marty corrected.

It was a powerful prayer. At the age of 44, not only am I pregnant, I'm overjoyed and so is the rest of the family. As for day-to-day physical needs, I have more maternity clothes now than for all my other five pregnancies combined. Once people realized I hadn't had the foresight to hang on to my maternity wear, they brought over boxes and bags of clothes. We've also been offered a cradle, a crib, and two car seats. As well, Marty got a good deal on a eight-seat mini-van. There isn't any doubt in my mind that this baby will be well-supplied and amply loved. *Thank you, Amanda, and thank you Lord.*

He fills his hands with lightning and commands it to strike its mark. (Job 36:32)

If Amanda hadn't said the prayers, would I be pregnant? I don't think so. Just as the lightning had to strike the chimney to cause the bricks to crumble, the prayers for a baby had to be said to be answered.

Saved by Grace

I think it was the lure of prizes that led me to suggest to three friends that we enter the third annual Calvin Christian School golf tournament. It didn't matter that I hadn't played more than six holes of golf in my life—my teammates were almost as unskilled. Besides, ladies were especially encouraged to come to this particular fund-raiser.

It didn't even matter that I would be about seven months pregnant during the tournament—I would simply have to bend over a little further on the swing to make sure my arms cleared my stomach.

The week before the September tournament we four women were quite prepared. We had arranged for an early tee-off time so as not to be playing in the heat of the day. Of course we would wear hats and bring along our sun-screen and plenty of golf balls.

Second Thoughts

Twelve hours before the big game my carefree attitude changed dramatically. I kept waking up throughout the night to the sound of the wind whistling outside the bedroom window. I heard rain. When I dozed I dreamt about a snow-covered golf course, about ducking flying golf balls, about climbing huge hills and walking miles up and down to tee-off locations that weren't there.

An hour before tee-off time I was still tossing about in bed. The phone rang; Marty answered. It was a teammate phoning to say she would be picking me up within 40 minutes and to bring a raincoat.

Obviously she hadn't read the front of the morning paper which headlined a warning about the tail-end of Hurricane Fran set to hit our area.

As I scurried around looking for rain gear large enough to cover my pregnant stomach, the phone rang again. By this time the rain was coming down in buckets. "You can go back to bed," the kindly voice on the line proclaimed. My relief was overwhelming. I was saved.

The organizers had decided simply to host the tournament dinner scheduled for that evening. At the dinner there would be a draw for the prizes. Each would-have-been participant would also receive a coupon to play the course some sunny time.

> *But he was pierced for our transgressions, he was crushed for our iniquities; the punishment that brought us peace was upon him, and by his wounds we are healed. (Isaiah 53:5)*

That evening Marty and I banqueted among friends in a large dry auditorium. There I was—enjoying a great meal and waiting for my number to be called so I could choose a prize even though I hadn't set foot on the golf course. It occurred to me that this is what it means to be saved by grace. When Jesus died on the cross for me, He went the 18 holes in the hurricane and I got the prize.

We Had Our Infants Baptized or Did We?

On Sunday we had little Elizabeth baptized. On Monday I had coffee with a friend who had just become a member of a Baptist church. For my friend to become a full member at that particular church required believer's baptism by immersion, even though 40 years earlier, her parents had seen to it that she was baptized by "sprinkling" as an infant.

My friend and I agreed there is no place in the Bible that actually says infants should or shouldn't be baptized.

So why did Marty and I have our Beth baptized on Sunday? One practical reason is that the church we belong to does it that way and we would rather not be kicked out. Another reason is we wanted Elizabeth to grow up loving and serving the Lord. We wanted to tell the Lord this. We also wanted fellow believers to know our desire, and we wanted their help. But mostly we wanted the Lord to receive Elizabeth as a covenant child.

According to our church, in having Elizabeth baptized, Marty and I acknowledged that she was born in sin and that Christ died for her. We also acknowledged the Bible as true and complete. And as parents we promised to do our best to bring her up to give her life to Jesus and to serve Him always.

Some of our friends and relatives wouldn't call what happened on Sunday baptism. They have a valid point. For them, baptism means Elizabeth has to believe and she has to choose. If Elizabeth was their child they would have a "dedication" (which is basically infant baptism without the water). Then they would add water to her "profession of faith" (which is her declaration of Jesus as Lord) and call that baptism.

I know that ultimately Elizabeth has to make her own decision for Christ, yet, I am glad I have the rich teaching about God's covenant family that my church provides. Then again, just because another denomination overlooks the covenant doesn't mean it doesn't exist for them. It's rather like two blindfolded acrobats on a high wire 50 metres above a big net. The Calvinist acrobat knows about the covenant net below. The other acrobat hasn't even heard about nets or what they are for. The acrobats collide and fall. Which one lands in the net? They both do.

God is an eternal God. His ways are higher than our ways. His net works whether we know about it or not. Nevertheless, He wants us all in every generation from every denomination to give ourselves to Him.

In celebration of the covenant, we invited our parents to share the infant baptism day with us; we appreciated all the people who congratulated us after the service, and we went to bed Sunday night feeling really blessed. Yes, Sunday, November 10, 1996, the day we acknowledged God's covenant seal on Elizabeth's life, was a very special day for our whole family. We pray that one day Elizabeth will make Him the Lord of her life. And, we'll celebrate with her if and when she wants to get baptized as a believer—like my friend who joined the Baptist Church.

> *So Paul asked, "Then what baptism did you receive?" "John's baptism," they replied. Paul said, "John's baptism was a baptism of repentance. He told the people to believe in the one coming after him, that is in Jesus." (Acts 19:3–4)*

I'm not saying infant baptism is equal to John's baptism. I'm simply suggesting John's baptism wasn't complete and neither is infant baptism.

Grounded in Christ

If you had been driving past our house just before noon that Monday before Christmas you would have seen Marty connecting a shiny new set of booster cables from our car to our van. You also would have seen me standing beside Marty reading instructions out of a vehicle owner's manual. If you had looked a little closer, you would have noticed my back slightly skewed to the right, and if you would have looked even closer you would have seen pain written on my face.

I had a backache I was trying to ignore. "Don't believe your symptoms, believe in the power of Jesus Christ to heal you," proclaimed the book on healing I had read.

"It isn't working!" my symptoms shouted as my lower back muscles tightened around the pain and my spine froze to the crooked angle of previous backaches.

But my sore back wasn't the only problem that morning. The van wouldn't start. One of the kids confessed to having left an interior light on after Marty had specifically asked her to turn it off on the way home from church the evening before. At least the dead battery problem seemed relatively easy to solve....

"Connect the red positive cable to the positive terminal of the vehicle with the dead battery." I read, "Connect the other end to the positive terminal of the good battery. Now connect the black negative cable to the good battery's negative terminal. The other end of the negative cable goes to a heavy, unpainted metal part of the vehicle with the dead battery."

Since there wasn't an unpainted part of the frame in the vicinity of the battery, and since my back ached, and since I am not always inclined to follow instructions to the letter, I told Marty to attach the cable to the painted hood latch.

While we waited for the charge to happen, we struck up a conversation with a neighbour, just as a friend pulled into our driveway. I hobbled over to see what my friend wanted. "I only have a minute. I've come to pray for your back," she said.

My friend and I retreated into the house as Marty and the neighbour tried to figure out why the van still wouldn't start. My friend put her hand on my back and prayed for healing.

After she left my back still ached, but my attention was drawn to a Bible verse: *Confess your sins to each other and pray for each other so that you may be healed. (James 5:16a)* This verse pricked my conscience. I knew immediately what sin I had been trying to cover up and ignore. It took me a day or so to get up the courage, but I did confess my sin to Marty and to my friend, and they each in turn prayed with me. (I'm not going to re-confess my sin on this page—it's been dealt with.)

> ...*as far as the east is from the west, so far has he removed our transgressions from us. (Psalm 103:12)*

When the unconfessed sin no longer stood between me and redemption and I was once more firmly grounded in Jesus Christ, the most amazing thing happened. A divine Chiropractor pulled, prodded and realigned my back. Soon my back was completely straight.

As for the van with the dead battery, when the neighbour and Marty grounded the negative black of the cable to an unpainted portion of the van frame, the motor roared to life.

The Lord is teaching me His ways through living parables. This is exciting and a little scary, but I'm sticking with Him.

Flying High

A cold sunny Sunday afternoon found Marty, myself and our two middle children, Paul and Michelle, cross-country skiing at the local golf course. We kept our heads down into the wind as we skied across the rolling landscape toward a tobogganing hill Michelle had discovered several days earlier. She led us to the crest of this giant hill where we stood anticipating a long exhilarating run, possibly right to the distant woods.

"You go first, Michelle," Marty said, thinking he'd give her the honour as this place was her discovery.

Michelle picked up the challenge, but took a tumble right in the middle of the slope.

Paul and Marty quietly discussed and pointed to the base of the hill as they patiently waited for Michelle to untangle herself. From under my wool hat I couldn't hear what they were saying. Anyway, I really didn't see the need for a discussion. It was a big hill. I could easily avoid Michelle. There was even a nice track several feet over from where Michelle had wiped out. I pushed off with my poles.

"Watch out for the ramps!" hollered Paul. His words blew away on the wind. I assumed he was yelling some kind of encouragement as I blindly followed the well-worn tracks down the slope. What a lovely hill! Then just as the ground started levelling out, I saw the ramp. It was a wide well-built ramp guaranteed to send any toboggan, sled or snowboard hurling through the air. I was within a ski length of this ramp when I noticed it. I was travelling too fast to bail out. It was too late to steer clear.

Now let me assure you, this 44-year-old woman is not a fearless wonder. I don't do ramps—if I know about them. I don't jump off diving boards or ride on roller coasters. Yet here I was flying through the air like Eddie the Eagle. I tried to line up my skis for a graceful landing but to no avail. The tips of my skis overlapped, and I ended in a jumbled heap on a patch of ice. That earned me some rather painful bruises on both knees and elbows.

> ...but God has revealed it to us by his Spirit. The Spirit searches all things, even the deep things of God. (1 Corinthians 2:10)

Looking back, I see that I address life much as I approached that hill. Just as I didn't see the need for a discussion with Marty and Paul about the hill; in life's decisions, often I don't wait for direction from the Holy Spirit. It's not possible to be Spirit-led if you don't listen. How can I even want what He wants without being in constant communication?

Mission-Trip Blues

When 18-year-old Angela signed up at church to spend two weeks with a 12-member mission team assigned to build a church and a parsonage in the Dominican Republic, her father and I were thrilled. When we found out our good friend Alice had signed up as well, we felt secure. And when Ann, another family friend and old-hand at mission trips, also promised to look out for Angela, we sent them all off with our prayers and blessings.

We looked forward to their return and their stories.

The first full day back, Angela didn't really have any stories. She didn't say much except, "I miss the group." She also didn't seem to notice that the cat and the baby had each grown about two inches. She hardly looked at them. Six-year-old Amanda (her dearest sister) put it bluntly when she called Angela a grump.

Late that afternoon my good friend Alice phoned.

"Hello, is Angela there?" she said.

"Alice, it's great to hear your voice again. How was it?" I enquired excitedly.

"Great! Listen I'm over at Ann's. We're looking at pictures."

"How's your nose? I heard you bumped it on a scaffold."

"Oh, it's fine. Is Angela there?"

Obviously Angela wasn't the only one who didn't want to talk to me. "I'll get her," I conceded.

I called up the stairs, "Angela, Alice is on the phone. She's at Ann's looking at pictures."

Angela burst out of her room, "I'll take it up here," she called as she flew to the phone.

Moments later she rushed downstairs with her recently developed wad of photos, "Mom, may I have the car to go over to Ann's?"

"Sure... but may I see a few pictures first?" I begged. I hadn't realized she had them back.

"Awwww, Mom."

She allowed me a peek at one group shot before she rushed out the door.

Feeling forsaken, the family started supper without Angela. Instead of a mealtime spent delighting in Angela's stories, as imagined, we moped. "She loves them more than us," fourteen-year-old Paul concluded.

The next day Ann phoned, "Is Angela there?"

"I won't attempt to engage you in small talk," I grumped. "I tried that with Alice...."

"...And she bit off your head," finished Ann.

"Well, not quite."

"It's like mourning," Ann explained. "You feel such a loss when you come back from one of these things. It's much like going through a death or a divorce."

Later I got a call from Marty's sister, "Is Marty there?"

I shared with her how the phone was never for me anymore. "The group is in mourning," I said.

As part of an ex-Wycliffe missionary family settled in Canada again after ten years in Papua New Guinea, she instantly identified. "So it happens after just two weeks too?"

That's when I got an inkling of her family's experience. "When you came back a year ago, it must have been a difficult adjustment." I said with new awareness.

"Yes! It still is," she stated.

> *But you will receive power when the Holy Spirit comes on you; and you will be my witnesses in Jerusalem, and in all Judea and Samaria, and to the ends of the earth. (Acts 1:8)*

Shouldn't the life of a Christian be one big meaningful mission trip?

This is the Day the Lord Has Made or A Day in the Life of a Homemaker

Tuesday morning I awoke promptly at 6:30 to the smell of bread baking in the bread-maker and the sound of the baby fussing in her crib. I shuffled down the hall to the baby's room. Little Elizabeth smiled winsomely as she arched around to greet me.

Sixteen and one quarter hours later at 10:45, I filled the bread-maker with ingredients and shuffled off to bed. My question is: Did anything in those 16 hours between emptying and filling my bread-maker produce fruit that would last?

I could rate my activities by how soon they would have to be repeated. Filling my cupboards with clean dishes from the dishwasher wouldn't have to be done again for another eight hours. Washing a load of baby Elizabeth's diapers was good for two days. Having the rugs shampooed and scotch-guarded would last up to a year.

On the other hand, something relational like my reaction to the question by the carpet-cleaning man when he heard baby noises, will possibly become what is called a lasting memory. "You have grandchildren here?" is not what this mother of a seven-month-old wanted to hear. I'm only 45. I told him rather pointedly that the baby was mine. He got embarrassed and mumbled something about his own grandchildren.

If I took an eternal measuring stick to the day, I would have to look at deeds done for others. What were my motives?

I like to think that each of the six times I fed the baby I did it out of love...or was it duty? And each of the half dozen times

I changed her diaper, I did it out of love...or was it necessity? Genuine love caused me to wave at my eldest daughter Angela on her way to work as our vehicles passed each other on the street...or was that pride? Surely, love motivated me to let Paul stay home from school. He was covered with an itchy rash. Or was my motivation fear that he would contaminate his school mates?

Love certainly didn't figure in as I spring cleaned behind the refrigerator. I did this to appease Marty who doesn't like dirt. Then again maybe I did it out of love for Marty. I finished designing a two-page newsletter on the computer simply for money, although I did enjoy doing it. (Was this love?)

I drove a neighbour who doesn't have a vehicle over to the Housing Authority so she could pay her rent. I did this because she asked—or was it because it made me feel good? Or was it love?

When Nora, whom I hadn't seen for 20 years, phoned me to invite our family to her parents' 50th wedding anniversary, I chatted for a quarter hour, I was genuinely interested in her family—or was I just nosey?

At the end of the day, all I can say is, "Lord, purify my heart." I want love to be my motivation and I want to be pure.

> *I appointed you to go and produce fruit that will last...I command you to love each other. (John 15:16b–17, New Living Translation)*

A friend read this description of my day and immediately felt sorry for me. It seemed to her I was striving to become acceptably righteous. That is not the case. God chose me; I don't have to earn His approval. I was merely examining my day for fruit that would last. I've been grafted into the vine. Now I want to produce plenty of excellent fruit.

As I complained to the Lord about my friend's misdirected pity, I heard Him say, "How do you think I feel when people misunderstand My book?"

Absence Makes the Heart Grow Fonder

When Marty first broached the subject of taking his widowed mom to Michigan for a week to visit her brothers, I thought it was a decent idea. It would be a good opportunity for him to get to know her better, and I could use the occasion to slack off—things wouldn't have to be quite so tidy around here, or meals so scheduled.

Settling the dates took some back and forth among all parties involved, but we finally came up with the second week in June. Marty was about to mark this on the calendar when he realized, "We can't do that. It'll be our wedding anniversary."

All the other weeks in June were already eliminated for one reason or another, and July was out of the question; so I urged him to go anyway. "We can always celebrate the anniversary when you come back," I observed. "It is only our 21st, not a 50th or a 25th."

So, on our 21st anniversary, when Marty had been gone for two days, I missed him. I hoped he missed me as much. It was the first time in 21 years we'd been apart on our anniversary. Originally I had thought the actual date wasn't all that important and we could celebrate by going out for a romantic candle-light dinner on the arranged Saturday night two weeks later. I didn't even send along a card for him to open. He didn't leave me one either.

At 9 o'clock on our anniversary morning he phoned. I was out. When I got back, I longed for him. I loved his lop-sided smile and when he winked at me. I loved the way I could tell him everything. I loved praying with him. I loved the way our kids reminded me of him, each in a different way. And now that he was away, I appreciated the way he tidied up after himself and the rest of us. The family room, now that he was away, was a mess—newspapers everywhere. The kids kept saying things like, "you can tell Dad's not here" and "this place is a mess."

I missed his kisses and having lunch together and topping his coffee with Josie's Famous Fruit Dip (a tasty creamy mixture manufactured by one of his clients).

Finally at five in the afternoon the phone rang again. "Happy anniversary, my love," came the familiar voice. He told me about the uncles and the cousins and the paddle boat and the turtles and I told him about the phone calls, the school newsletter, the kids' soccer games, and opening our pool.

That evening Angela and I went shopping. We bought bathing suits, shorts and shirts and I bought a dress. Marty wouldn't recognize me when he came back.

It wasn't such a bad anniversary after all, and I still had that romantic candle-light dinner to look forward to. I even tidied the family room before I went to bed.

> *One thing I ask of the Lord, this is what I seek: that I may dwell in the house of the Lord all the days of my life, to gaze upon the beauty of the Lord and to seek him in his temple. (Psalm 27:4)*

When Marty left I anticipated a joy in being free from his orderly "accountant" ways. I was wrong. I didn't enjoy the mess. Similarly I don't enjoy stepping outside the love of Christ by deliberately walking in sin. With Marty on my heart, I couldn't help but do things that would please him. By the same token, if Jesus is on my heart, I am Christ-centred.

The Parable of the Window Seat

"I don't sew," I explained to the fabric store clerk who asked if I had a sewing club card. Then why was I standing there with two spools of heavy duty brown thread, a packet of sewing machine needles marked *leather*, and five yards of Quaker upholstery material in a floral design?

Marty's new part-time employee sews. That is why I could so confidently make these purchases. If I ran stuck, she would be able to set me straight. It's not that I don't know anything about sewing. I do own a sewing machine—for mending mostly. Years ago I took a few basic sewing courses at which time I put together a pair of grey slacks (worn only once) and a red floral shirt I still wear when I want to paint something. Over the years I've also experimented on drapes and curtains with varying degrees of success.

This was to be my most ambitious sewing project to date. I was planning to re-upholster the window seat in the south window of the family room. The window seat was a well-made sturdy bench originally covered in a wine-red geometric pattern. This covering had faded to a dull pink and was literally pulling apart at the seams. I thought of throwing an afghan over the bench, but imagined myself straightening it every time the cat, the baby or a teenager walked into the room which would probably be once every twelve minutes. So much for that idea.

When I brought home my $37.50-worth of upholstery material, nobody jumped up and down about my choice. "It goes real well with the carpet" was the most positive remark the family could come up with. (I didn't remind them that we were changing the carpet.) Allison thought the old stars and geometric shapes far superior to these brown and orange flowers. Paul preferred the smooth texture of the original fabric. "This is like lying on a rug," he commented as he sprawled across the new material.

Marty's secretary showed me how to overlap the fabric at the corners and gave me some advice about placing flowers strategically to create the illusion of a matched pattern.

With that and the suggestions by the lady at the store to use the biggest stitch on the machine and set a very loose tension on the thread, I was only four prayers, eighteen hours, three needles and one trip back to the store for more thread, away from a finished product.

Now the bench looks fresh and new. I can't stop admiring my handiwork. Too bad the kids don't like it. "The old is better," they say.

> "...No one tears a patch from a new garment and sews it on an old one....no one pours new wine into old wineskins....And no one after drinking old wine wants the new, for he says, 'The old is better.'"(Luke 5:36–39)

Am I blooming yet? To truly bloom, I need to wear the new garment and drink from the new wineskin. The old garment was more comfortable. The rules and rituals held everything in place. This new Holy Spirit clothing feels unfamiliar. Carpet-time, speaking in tongues, falling down under the anointing—at times I want to say, "The old is better!"—more stable, predictable, explainable. But God is doing a new thing and this calls for a new wineskin.

The Parable of the Direction Sheet

Flub-flup-flub-fluppity-flup-flup.

"Pull over right here," I directed Allison, our student-driver daughter. Allison brought the family van to a halt. We were blocking the inside lane of traffic on Upper Paradise Road during rush hour on a chilly autumn afternoon. As Allison fumbled for the two-way flashers, I stepped out to discover our rear right tire was completely flat.

Since we were less than a kilometre from home, Michelle and Amanda didn't waste any time. "May we walk home?"

"Tell Dad to come help me here," I called as they headed up the sidewalk.

Allison entertained Elizabeth while I opened the rear van door and unlatched the side panel marked "Jack." The pocket behind the panel was filled with tire-changing apparatus including a tire-changer's bible in the form of a laminated direction sheet on a plastic ring permanently attached to the van.

The instructions appeared rather convoluted so I decided to rely on my tire-changing experience which consisted mostly of watching other people change tires. I set the jack and jack handle beside each other under the van frame behind the wheel. There were arrows on the handle. I was still discerning between up and down when a strolling couple stopped.

"My husband should be coming along soon," I said. The man picked up the jack parts and easily assembled them. "It looks like your husband will have to place the jack under the axle because it won't work where you have it," he discreetly remarked before continuing on his way.

Where was Marty? The steel of the jack was cold on my hands.

"May I take Elizabeth home?" asked Allison.

"Sure and find out what happened to Dad."

After searching under all the seats I found the spare tire securely mounted under the body of the van. Now I could no longer avoid reading the instructions. I was supposed to stick the chisel end of the jack handle through the hole in the cargo door frame to wind down the spare tire.

What hole? I didn't see any hole. The accompanying diagram didn't look at all like reality. I poked the chisel end of the handle under the van, rather like waving an awkward magic wand, hoping to land it in a hole somehow. I reread the instructions. Then I opened the second cargo door. There was the hole in the frame, right where it was supposed to be.

After finally dismounting the spare, I tried to loosen the wheel nuts on the flat tire with the wrench end of the jack handle. I tried each nut using all my strength but nothing budged.

Just as it was growing dark, Marty drove up, strode over and smiled, "I would have been here sooner but Michelle and Amanda forgot all about you."

He loosened the nuts with his superior strength, placed the jack under the axle and in short order the tire was changed. I headed home with Marty's car, and he took the tire to the local garage.

> *All Scripture is God-breathed and is useful for teaching, rebuking, correcting and training in righteousness, so that the man of God may be thoroughly equipped for every good work. (2 Timothy 3:16–17)*

The Bible is like a direction sheet: the more we study it, the clearer it becomes. It doesn't give us a magic wand to be waved about indiscriminately but does provide indispensable information. Putting the Word into action accurately, works every time. The superior power of the Holy Spirit also helps.

The Parable of the Firemen

The morning newscast set off alarm bells in my head: *family dies...carbon monoxide poisoning...low grade flu...older gas appliance.*

Older gas appliance...we possessed a second-hand *harvest gold* gas range which for ten years had served us faithfully and who knows who else for the 30 odd years before that.

Low grade flu... a normally healthy child was sprawled out in the family room with flu-like symptoms: dizzy, tired, headachy and nauseous.

I lifted the burner pans on the range to check the pilot lights. One of the lights was hardly burning. I scraped away some white sediment with a bread knife. The flame brightened. I opened the kitchen patio door. Fresh January air filled the room.

An hour later when I heard the poisoning news repeated along with a story about dead snowmobilers who hadn't heeded thin-ice *warnings*, I decided to call the gas company. They could check my range and set my mind at ease.

The gas company receptionist took down all the information and made an appointment for a gas man to see me in 48 hours. Then she had a revelation, "This possibly calls for the fire department."

Within seconds I was in a three-way conversation with the gas company and the fire department, "We'll send a truck over right away!"

What had I done? We certainly didn't need a fire truck. Quickly I ran downstairs to Marty's office; "Uhh, Marty...a fire truck will be here any minute." I told him what had transpired making it sound as mundane as possible.

Within minutes we could hear the sirens approaching. The next thing I knew, my kitchen was filled with seven huge firemen, a mass of yellow, orange and black. They made me think of angels—calm and ready for any emergency. Fourteen-month-old Elizabeth stared up at them with her big brown eyes, not the least bit frightened.

A spokesman asked about circumstances, other gas appliances and whether we had a carbon monoxide tester. I had never heard of such a thing. It seems you plug the tester into an outlet and it beeps like a smoke detector if there is an unacceptable level of carbon monoxide in the air.

The fireman asked me about our little kitchen gadget that looked to him like a carbon monoxide tester.

"Oh that emits a high pitched screech to make life unpleasant for rodents. It's one of those things you kind of wonder about—does it really work or are they pulling one over on me?" I told him I bought it because I didn't want to set traps or use poison because we have a cat.

"If you have a cat you shouldn't need traps."

"He's declawed."

The firemen tramped through the house checking our gas furnace and water heater as well. They gave the place a carbon monoxide-free rating and asked me to sign a form verifying the work. I thanked them all and sheepishly asked if I could take a picture. Not a one responded to the request, so I dropped it. I don't think it's possible to take a picture of angels—even though I know they are as real as those firemen.

Are not all angels ministering spirits sent to serve those who will inherit salvation? (Hebrews 1:14)

Just as my one simple phone call resulted in seven firemen in my kitchen, one little prayer can bring God's angels onto the scene.

The Parable of the Membership Card

For several days a "Service Engine Soon" message had been flashing at me sporadically from the dashboard of the family minivan. At first I took it seriously, but after a while I convinced myself there was something wrong with the message; the van was running perfectly.

Then one fine day on the way back from a morning of running errands all over Hamilton from Ancaster to Stoney Creek, the van hesitated, clunked and died. I was just able to coast around the corner to a stop on a quiet side street.

I tried restarting the engine, but the smoke, smell and noises convinced me to lock up, and since I was only a kilometre away, to walk home.

I didn't personally hold an Automobile Association membership card, but Marty did so I took his card and phoned the association. The person there said she would send someone around within the hour.

Because I told her I was using my husband's card, she queried, "Is your husband there?"

"Yes, he is." I didn't tell her he was up to his eyeballs in work.

"Good, because the cardholder has to be with the vehicle or you might be charged for the tow."

At the height of tax season, my accountant husband was hardly ready to sit waiting for a tow truck. We decided I would wait for the truck and call Marty only when and if necessary. Armed with excuses, I took the card and my favourite book, the Bible, over to the site of the disabled van. In just about an hour a tow truck showed up. The driver was more interested in getting his job done than whether my husband was actually physically present at the towing. With speed and efficiency he hooked up the van and was off to the garage.

Back behind the wheel, a few days and $400 later, with Marty's association card once again in my possession, I headed to the Automobile Association headquarters. This time I intended to use his card to pick up maps and information on the Niagara area for a weekend getaway. After the tax season Marty and I like to get reacquainted.

The attendant at the counter informed me that it doesn't work to use someone else's card, even if it's your husband. Then she kindly gave me information, photocopies, phone numbers—everything I asked for and more.

> *Therefore, it is necessary to submit to the authorities, not only because of possible punishment but also because of conscience. (Romans 13:5)*

As I think about it, I realize if I use the services of the Automobile Association I should abide by their rules. They are the authority in this case. My maverick attitude is simply not Christian.

Looking further, I see this same attitude reflected in my relationship with my denomination. I don't agree with everything taught, yet I claim the benefits of membership. Is that a "service engine soon" message I see flashing?

Fly the Cat and Making Sacrifices

Early one evening, our bald-headed neighbour with the big moustache who lives three doors down, came knocking, "Is yours the little black and white cat?" he asked.

"Yes," I admitted proudly.

"Well, the neighbours would appreciate it if you kept him as an indoor cat."

My neighbour proceeded to tell me exactly what our cat Fly had been doing. It seems Fly had an outdoor routine to which we, his family, were oblivious. He would walk up to the door two houses over and paw against it until he had the little dog inside running in circles barking. Then Fly would head over to our moustached neighbour's house and do the same thing for his dog.

Fly's biggest crime took place six houses down the street. The lady there spent many delightful hours attracting birds to her yard. She fed them and could boast of attracting a whole array of birds including cardinals. It seems Fly would crouch behind her bushes. He actually murdered one of her doves.

"Our cat doesn't even have claws!" I exclaimed to the neighbour with the big moustache. "We had no idea. We certainly don't want him making a nuisance of himself."

I decided then and there to keep Fly inside. Within two days I was rethinking my decision. If Fly happened to be within streaking distance of an opening door, chances were he'd escape and one of us would be up to five minutes recapturing him. When we managed to keep him housebound for more than half a day, he honed his stalking skills ambushing our ankles.

I began letting Fly out the back door for short periods during the middle of the day.

"Maybe he only does the dog and bird routine in the evening," I mused. "Or maybe he won't go down the street if I let him out a different door. Doesn't the cat have a right to go outside? Is there a bylaw against it?"

I know I should talk to my neighbours about this. I should at least make amends with the bird lady. But I'm probably not going to.

The sacrifices of God are a broken spirit; a broken and contrite heart, O God, you will not despise. (Psalm 51:17)

The way I'm trying to appease my neighbours from a distance, without talking to them, reminds me of the way I often relate to God. Even though I want to walk as the Holy Spirit directs, I can get quite comfortable making imperfect sacrifices. I'll just do what seems reasonable and necessary for appearances. *O God, help me!*

A Dogma Dies

Dogma: a specific doctrine or tenet authoritatively put forth.

I was brought up believing that liver is good for you. My parents said liver was a healthy food, and with even more authority my physics teacher in high school declared it was the most nutritious of all foods. My physics teacher told us that he had eaten liver religiously every day for a month and benefited greatly. His son—who I'm sure ate liver as well—went on to participate in the Olympic games in the diving competition.

Then one day Allison came home from high school proclaiming liver is not good to eat. Her family-studies teacher reasoned that the liver traps and processes impurities that pass through the body. When you eat liver, the impurities in that liver go to your liver.

This reasoning sounded pretty good to my family because they don't like liver. I like liver so I stuck to the dogma expressed by my physics teacher. But alas, with the family-studies teacher on their side it became harder and harder for me to serve liver to my family.

Yet, one particular day, fully keyed up to overcome all objections, I intended to cook the slab of liver that had been staring me in the face every time I opened the freezer.

"What are we having for supper, Mom?"

"Liver," I boldly proclaimed, "*My Children Love Liver*, the finger food recipe."

"No! No! Nooooooo!" came a chorus of protests.

Michelle wanted to argue so I offered her the opportunity to make us something else. She declined as I thought she would.

"Cheryl and I don't like liver," Amanda stated.

"Well Cheryl doesn't have to stay," I suggested looking at Amanda's friend.

"But she wants to."

"Then she'll have to eat at least two pieces, just as you will," I pronounced.

"What are we having with it?" asked Allison, hopefully.

"Spinach," I declared, thinking I'd make it a truly memorable meal.

Allison and Michelle suddenly found it within their budget to satisfy an overwhelming desire to eat pizza together at the local mall.

Cheryl and Amanda ate their two pieces of liver with their little fingers on their noses bringing a new definition to finger food. Then they had peanut butter sandwiches.

Baby Elizabeth spit her liver out as fast as I could spoon it in. I made a sandwich for her as well.

Marty on the other hand, ate with such gusto I dared ask him to rate the meal on a scale from one to ten.

"Three," he said decisively.

"One," chimed in fifteen-year-old Paul.

"But, you ate with such enthusiasm?"

"A put-on for the benefit of the children," Marty explained.

It was at this point my dogma died. I now sincerely believe liver is not a good food to serve at *our* house.

> "Woe to you experts in the law, because you have taken away the key to knowledge...." (Luke 11:52a)

Church doctrines can be compared to liver. They are intended to trap and process spiritual impurities, but as Allison's teacher taught, "When you eat liver, the impurities in that liver go to your liver." I'd better stick with pure Bible.

Enough Already!

It costs a bundle to park at the hospital downtown—eight dollars per day if you spend any amount of time there. Marty and I had been spending a lot of time there visiting our Allison who was being treated for depression.

Probably because we are Dutch, we decided not to use the expensive hospital lot, but to park in available spots along nearby side streets. This turned out to be not as simple as it sounds.

The City of Hamilton has some very complicated rules about parking on the streets particularly in the vicinity of the hospital. These rules are all spelled out on red and white signs, inside parking meters and on yellow stickers attached to the meter posts. They are spelled out in even greater detail on the six-section parking tickets that we too frequently found flapping about under the windshield wiper of our parked vehicle.

The night we brought Allison in, Marty parked the car beside a parking meter. It was late Monday evening well *after the 6 p.m. Monday, Tuesday and Wednesday* when a person no longer has to feed the meter. But when we got back to the car at about 3 a.m. there was this red, green and white ticket envelope on our windshield. We were being fined $30 (early payment $20) for parking on a through street between 2 a.m. and 7 a.m. How could we have missed it? There it was—in plain black and yellow small bold capital letters halfway down the parking meter post—NO PARKING BETWEEN 2 A.M. AND 7 A.M.

We've also been fined $20 for parking at a meter which we faithfully fed while neglecting to read the sign about *no parking between 4 p.m. and 6 p.m.* Then there was the $20 fine I was given while parked at a sign proclaiming *three hour parking*. I didn't see the sign right beside it that said FIRE ROUTE, no parking.

We've become very careful, but sometimes it doesn't seem to make a difference. Take the time I went to visit Allison for the afternoon. I was somewhat later than I said I would be, so I was quite delighted when I found a spot within close range of the hospital doors. In fact I thanked the Lord for letting me have such a good spot right under a shady tree next to a big red mailbox. I pulled into the spot and three times I read the sign right outside my van window. It said *3 hour parking* with arrows pointing both ways. I checked the curb to be sure I wasn't blocking any driveways.

Secure in the fact that I was legally parked, I spent an enjoyable afternoon with Allison who was doing quite well.

When I returned, the ticket I found under my wiper came as a total surprise. *Set fine $75, early payment $50 for parking within 10 feet of a hydrant.* As an added touch the ticketing officer had noted along the edge of the ticket in pen in capital letters "COMPLETE OBSTRUCTION OF HYDRANT AT REAR BUMPER." Sure enough there was the bright red hydrant next to the mailbox.

By now we've paid the City of Hamilton much more than we would have paid the hospital if we had used the lot. Yet we must be beggars for punishment because we still insist on parking in the streets with the mish-mash of rules—just because we're Dutch.

Our most recent fine was $8 for having exceeded paid time at a meter. Actually we didn't feed the meter because it was after 6 p.m., not realizing that the day was Thursday when you have to put money in the meter until 9 p.m.

Sometimes all you can do is laugh.

Obey your leaders and submit to their authority. They keep watch over you as men who must give an account. Obey them so that their work will be a joy, not a burden, for that would be of no advantage to you. (Hebrews 13:17)

Our parking dilemma parallels our spiritual situation. If we choose to park at the hospital, the rules are clear, we pay a maximum of $8 per day. If we choose to park out in the streets, it's up to us to read the signs correctly or pay the penalty. If we're members of a church we accept the doctrines of that place. And if we go against the direction of our spiritual leadership (which we have) we also lose the spiritual protection of that leadership. It would be better for our family if we could stop being mavericks.

Cooking in Faith

When I happily agreed to accept two grocery bags full of red ripe tomatoes on Sunday evening, I knew on Monday morning I would be making tomato sauce to freeze in recipe-sized portions for the weeks ahead. But I didn't know what I would be using as freezer containers. I usually reuse plastic yogurt tubs, but the few I had left after strawberry season I had already used for the tomato sauce I had made the week before. Our family goes through a lot of tomato sauce.

As I cut up my tomatoes, peppers and onions, I reflected on the sermon on faith I'd heard on Sunday. The preacher said that faith is a substance to live by. Noah, Abraham and Moses lived by faith. Jesus said if you prayed in faith you could move a mountain. That's why I wasn't the least bit concerned about how I would freeze my sauce. I had prayed in faith and confidently expected something I could use.

When I had four large pans of sauce simmering on the stove, Marty who knew what I lacked, came into the kitchen. "So what are you going to freeze your sauce in?"

"I don't know yet. I prayed for containers."

"But you need something now!"

"Not quite. The sauce has to simmer."

While waiting for my vessels to materialize I had the thought to call my friend Helen and tell her what I was doing.

"I've got lots of those plastic yogurt containers."

"You don't need them?"

"I was planning to give them away."

"I'll be right over."

After I hung up, I found Marty in his office. "I'm going to pick up my containers. They're at Helen's house."

He sighed, "Why didn't you tell me? You made it sound like you didn't know where they were coming from."

"I didn't."

"Well you should have thought of asking Helen before you started the sauce."

"I prayed instead. 'Faith is the substance of things not seen,'" I misquoted.

He shook his head.

Over at Helen's, she pointed to a stack of empty yogurt tubs and three margarine containers she had ready on her kitchen table, "I can give you more if you need them."

I fingered the vessels and thought of the four pans of sauce bubbling on my stove, "Three, six, nine, twelve—looks about right."

Back home I ladled out my sauce beginning from the largest pan. Because it occurred to me that I might run short I filled each tub nearly to the top, leaving very little head room. I hoped the lids wouldn't pop off as the sauce froze.

When all the pans were empty I had one empty margarine tub left. "I should have known," I thought as I scooped a bit out of each too-full container.

> Now faith is being sure of what we hope for and certain of what we do not see. (Hebrews 11:1)

This "cooking in faith" episode is a picture of faith at work. We have a need. We pray. We believe. God meets the need with perfection and perfect timing.

That Still Small Voice

In hindsight I should have used the sun screen. I shouldn't have eaten that extra sausage. I should have put more air in the air mattress. And I should have moved the van away from the edge of the street. In fact, I should have obeyed that oh-so-sensible still small voice.

On a beautiful sunny morning at Darien Lake I did remember to apply sun screen to my sun-sensitive nose, but at noon when a thought to reapply the sun screen passed through my mind, I didn't do it. It's just so peaceful to be at lunch and not get up for anything—ask any mother of six kids who is away on a camping holiday with her husband and just one of their children.

At suppertime I fried up a package of five sausages on our trusty camp stove. We feasted on creamed corn, applesauce and cheese-filled sausages on buns. Marty had two sausages, I had one, and Michelle had one. The sensible thought was to wrap the extra sausage in tin foil and share it for breakfast. I ate it instead.

Then after a fun-filled evening as we were bedding down in the tent I realized that my side of the air mattress felt a little soft. I remembered Marty mentioning how the previous night he had awakened every time he rolled over because his part of the mattress was too soft. I accused him of turning the mattress over, but that's another story. Good sense told me to blow up the air mattress before going to sleep. Nah, I vetoed that. I was too cosy and tired, and instead, snuggled down into the double sleeping bag.

Sure enough I woke up every time I rolled over. But it took four wake-ups before I actually crawled out of the sleeping bag to do what I should have done much earlier. Back in the sack, wide-awake, I realized my stomach ached—that extra sausage, maybe? Also my nose hurt; felt sort of burned.

Now one would think that with these three fine examples of what happens when I don't listen to that sensible, still small voice I would change my ways. But sometimes I need a hard-hitting example.

The clincher came a few days later while I was waiting in our van in a pick-up area at the front of a building along Hamilton's Main Street, waiting for Allison. As a bus crept by within inches of my driver's-side window I realized the van was a tad close to the traffic whizzing along Main Street.

"Back up into the empty space behind you, it's safer," said that still small voice. "It's not worth it; Allison will be here any minute," argued my lazy self.

Not three minutes later, the time it would have taken me to start the van and back into the spot behind me, a pickup truck flew by and I heard a thud. I looked out at my side mirror. The glass was cracked into a dozen pieces. That cost me $25 and 30 minutes at Standard Glass.

By faith Noah, when warned about things not yet seen, in holy fear built an ark to save his family. By his faith he condemned the world and became heir of righteousness that comes by faith. (Hebrews 11:7)

Lord, help me obey your still small voice. In former days I would have chalked up my error to stupidity. Now I know it is disobedience.

Where is the Life Jacket?

The events of the day were determined when little Elizabeth followed me to the edge of the pool that fine spring morning and quietly reminded me about "that thing I put on," but I ignored her. The previous year we had insisted she always wear a life jacket within the vicinity of the pool.

Maybe it was her caution that lulled me into feeling secure. Besides, I couldn't remember where I had stored the life jacket. "We'll have to look for that, later," I said. Meanwhile, I continued vacuuming a layer of leaves from the bottom of the pool. The pool seemed in good shape this year. It helped that I knew what I was doing. I already had two-thirds of the vacuuming done. The filter was set on "drain" to send this spring debris directly to the sewer and I had a hose with fresh clean water pouring into the pool at the shallow end—a hose which Elizabeth leaned over to examine. "Be careful," I cautioned. About then I noticed my vacuum had stopped sucking. I examined the vacuum head, then decided to check the filter basket at the pump inside the garage. I didn't see Elizabeth. I didn't even think about Elizabeth.

Sure enough the filter basket in the garage was completely clogged. I turned off the pump, pulled out the several handfuls of leaves and started the system up again. Suddenly I remembered Elizabeth. I ran back to the pool in a panic. There she was in the middle of the pool, like a rag doll floating face down. I jumped in and scooped her up, screaming for help. Angela and Allison appeared immediately.

"Call 911! Get Dad!" I commanded. By the time I had Elizabeth to the edge of the pool, Marty was there to perform

CPR as if it was something he did every day. I prayed in tongues. It was all I could do. I was in shock.

Within minutes the paramedics arrived. Taking charge, they said we had done all the right things. Full of guilt, I knew that not making the life jacket a priority hadn't been the right thing at all.

At the hospital nurses took Elizabeth into a room and cut away her little flowered dress. A team of specialists surrounded her. We sat in a waiting area, praying. Pastor Sharon from church prayed with us. She prayed that Elizabeth's lungs would be whole and well. She prayed that her brain would not be damaged. She prayed that I wouldn't carry the guilt.

Shortly after that a doctor talked to us. He spoke of possible damage to the lungs. He spoke of a likelihood of brain damage. We told him we had prayed and were believing for those things not to happen.

The next day the doctor approached us, "Well, it looks like you got your miracle. The brain scan shows no damage." We were elated. Further tests showed that her lungs were clear as well.

On Saturday evening when we finally had Elizabeth home, tucked in bed, Marty and I were relaxing with a coffee in the family room. "I wouldn't want to go through a week like that, again," I reflected. Marty agreed.

Was that Elizabeth crying upstairs? Then the door bell rang. I went for the stairs while Marty answered the door.

"Your baby is on the roof!" announced the neighbour at the door. Sure enough Elizabeth had let herself down from the bedroom window onto the latticed deck roof.

I never want to go through a week like that again.

> *The words "it was credited to him (Abraham)" were written not for him alone, but also for us, to whom God will credit righteousness—for us who believe in him who raised Jesus our Lord from the dead. (Romans 4:23—24)*

Grace, the grace of God, is what saved us that week. My own righteousness was as limp as a rag doll in the middle of a pool. By His righteousness we could pray and believe for life and health for our little girl. By His grace He answered.

Am I blooming yet? Yes, because I let Him cut away my flowery dress of self-righteousness and His righteousness has become mine.

The Heads of the House

Because you have made the Lord your refuge, and the Most High your dwelling place, there shall no evil befall you, nor any plague or calamity come near your tent. (Psalm 91:9—10, Amplified)

What was I doing wrong? At first it was every few years, then at least once a year, and finally one year, every six or seven weeks at least one of my children would begin scratching her head causing the pit of my stomach to sink.

"Come to the window," I would groan and the child would moan as I once again checked for head lice. As often as not I would find one or more tiny black parasites crawling across a blonde child's scalp or see the minute white eggs attached to a brunette child's hairs.

I fought these insidious insects with an arsenal of weapons in the natural and in the spiritual. In the natural I tried every louse shampoo on the market. I religiously followed the directions on the lice-battle-sheets the kids brought home from school. I bought the special, metal nit-comb. I carefully removed each individual nit. I boiled combs and brushes until they were warped and useless. I washed bedding, sprayed and turned mattresses, wrapped stuffed animals in plastic bags, sprayed furniture and van seats, and washed coats and scarves and hoods. I obediently informed the school. I suffered the embarrassment of warning friends and relatives who might have been exposed to the heads of our children. The pharmacist began to know me as the lady with the ongoing head-lice problem.

I assumed the Lord was teaching me humility, patience and endurance. Eventually I could do the whole delousing routine in one morning and still have energy left to meet the rest of the day.

On the spiritual front, I prayed over my children's heads. I called several friends to pray with me. We prayed the lice to die in Jesus' name. I read Psalm 91 every day for a month to increase my faith. I prayed Psalm 91, believing every word.

Where was Marty in this? Well, this was my territory. Then one evening at the video Bible School Marty and I attended, we learned about the husband as priest of the household taking spiritual responsibility. Our Bible School teacher talked about unanswered prayer and the need to "find the lack and trace it to the slack." In the case of the lice, not only was Marty not taking the spiritual responsibility, I hadn't seen it as necessary, or even helpful—I had read more books than he had about spiritual warfare.

In the course of time, lice broke out again. This time Marty and I and the girls prayed together as family. I tried to rest in the Lord under Marty's headship, but it wasn't working. I noticed Elizabeth scratching her head. My own head itched. I woke up at night worrying about lice.

I woke Marty to share my dilemma. That's when the Holy Spirit led us in confessing the root of the problem. I repented for thinking myself as more spiritual than Marty and we both confessed our wrong attitudes. My relief was tangible. I was at peace.

In the morning Elizabeth's hair was a mess. I combed it, but it wouldn't stay down. I saw her scratching her head. Not wanting even the appearance of doing something wrong, I went straight to my husband, who was already at his desk in the basement totally engrossed in his day's work. I apologized, "Normally I would take care of this, but..." I got to the point. "I saw Elizabeth scratching her head and I'm thinking about lice again. What shall I do?" He looked at me. Was that a sigh? "Check her head," he said blandly.

I did—and yes, her head was full of lice—dead ones!

Wives, submit to your husbands as to the Lord. For the husband is the head of the wife as Christ is the head of the church, his body, of which he is the Savior. (Ephesians 5:22–23)

I would like to say we never again had to deal with lice. I would also like to say I now perfectly and always line up with Marty, the spiritual head of the house. But that would be lying. Let's just say the incidents are fewer and farther between—now that we recognize the slack.

The Holy Spirit is a superb guide. Slowly and steadily He is changing the way I see myself and the way I relate to others.

Football Foul-up

"A client gave us two tickets to the football game Friday. Do you want to come?" asked Marty.

"Okay," I said, although I wasn't exactly a football fan. We hadn't been to a professional football game since our courtship some 28 years past. But I did like the idea of a Friday night out with my husband.

"It's a date then." He smiled with boyish pleasure.

On the way to the game Marty told me more about the tickets, "One is for a kid and one is for a senior. We'll probably have to pay the difference."

Even though I'm half a year older than Marty he took the senior ticket because "I have the gray hair," he explained. This made me feel younger than I had in a long time.

The game had already started as we stragglers proceeded through the turnstiles. The ticket-taker didn't even look at them as she ripped our tickets and handed back the stubs.

We were in. Someone gave us programs and Marty went over to the concession stand to buy coffee and juice.

As I waited for Marty my conscience kicked in. Marty and I had been caught in deception. Ordinarily I could handle this type of situation with some rationalization. Not this time and I knew why. All week I had been praying and meditating about seeking God's face and desiring to be in His presence continually.

I quietly followed Marty to our bench seats in section 30 near the end field and row J halfway up the bleachers.

I had trouble picking out the ball. Maybe I needed stronger glasses. As well, I was distracted by the many fanatical fans in an array of costumes, the loud noises, strange football customs and of course my guilty conscience not to mention the cold wind which gusted up every few minutes, blowing debris in circles around us.

"I shouldn't have left my jacket in the car," I said shivering.

Marty offered to go to the car for me but I insisted on getting the jacket myself. I thought I could possibly straighten out my ticket problem at the same time.

"Going home?" asked the girl at the turnstile.

"No, just to the car for my jacket."

"Sorry, we won't be able to let you back in once you are out."

That killed that idea. "I have another problem," I confessed. "Someone gave us our tickets, and mine is a kid ticket...I'm not a kid," I said, feeling very much like one.

The girl smiled at me, "Nothing we can do about that now, just don't let an official in a yellow jacket see that ticket."

I spent the second half looking for officials in yellow jackets, wishing I had a jacket and attempting to ease my conscience. My scattered thoughts included: *I'm only understanding as much about this game as a kid would; I'm too cold to enjoy this game anyway;* and *the football people are glad to have us here for statistical purposes* (about a quarter of the seats were empty).

The game ended 17–11 for the visitors.

At home, I confessed to Marty, "I felt guilty the whole time...being a kid."

"Huh?"

"Having a kid's ticket."

"The tickets were given to us."

"So!"

"You could send them the money."

"That isn't the answer. I have to be right with God."

> *But your iniquities have separated you from your God; your sins have hidden his face from you, so that he will not hear. (Isaiah 59:2)*

I repented. So did Marty. Jesus had already paid for this sin...*whoever confesses and forsakes his sins will obtain mercy. (Proverbs 28:13b, Amplified)*. Thank you Lord.

By repenting and accepting Jesus' payment for my sin, I put myself back into His righteousness and, yes, His presence came flooding back.

Telephone Trap

I don't wish to be rude. I don't want to be a poor steward. I don't want to be bamboozled. But, just about every day, usually near the supper hour, I had an opportunity to be tested in each of these areas.

A bur in my flesh, the telephone appeal for funds, had been working to prove to me that I was rude, unloving, selfish, fearful, a poor steward and/or easily deceived. My usual way to deal with these calls was to avoid them.

"Ringgg."

"Hello, Marian speaking."

No immediate response. During that pause before the telemarketing apparatus finished what it was doing, I would hang up. If I slipped up on avoidance, sometimes I would impatiently tell the caller I had more important things to do (not a lie) and then I would hang up. Sometimes I would pretend politeness and semi-listen to the spiel. At the final pause I would say, "I don't think so," and hang up.

Or I would cause a stalemate by saying, "Send me the information."

"Sorry we can't do that without a pledge."

"Sorry, I can't help you."

But these telephone conversations always left me feeling less than Christian.

How could I know the organization phoning me was legitimate? I could make a blanket rule never to give by phone. I could give to no one. I couldn't give to everyone.

I prayed, "God, I need wisdom." Now according to James 1:5-6 that is a prayer He would answer if I prayed it in faith.

With this I was armed to handle the phone calls. Where once I became angry, frustrated, annoyed, rude or impatient, now I would ask the Holy Spirit for help and then listen with my inner ear. I would expect God to inform me if it was wise to give and even how much to give. Jesus always had wise answers for the Pharisees. He could always see past their words into their motives. Shouldn't I expect the same, after all He gave me the indwelling Holy Spirit as a guide.

"But, Jesus was perfect and walked in perfection," my brain argued. And thanks to Him so can I according to Hebrews 10:14...*because by one sacrifice he has made perfect forever those who are being made holy.*

With this awareness of who I was in Christ, leaning entirely on Him, I answered my next call.

"Hello this is ADT Digital Security System. You are eligible for a 10 to 15 minute presentation anytime Monday to Saturday. Mom and Dad authorized me—"

"Pardon? Who authorized you?" I broke in as I turned off my CD player.

"My manager authorized me."

"Where are you from?"

"Home Security Systems. We offer free installation."

"Why would I want it? We already have a security system."

"You have electronic surveillance?"

"No, actually we pray and we trust the Lord to take care of us."

"Okay then, thank you very much." Click.

This could be fun. The Lord has awakened a longing in me to tell others about Him. If I stay tuned, I'm sure He'll continue to give me creative opportunities.

Cat

"Do you think this could possibly be about your cat?" Terry, my next-door neighbour, sheepishly handed me an unaddressed letter. "The neighbour back there," he pointed across his backyard, "gave it to me. I told her I didn't own a cat and from her description I don't think it's your cat either."

I took the letter from his hand. It read in part:

I am writing this letter on behalf of some of your neighbours. We have witnessed your cat...on our properties many, many times in the past. We have contacted the City and had a by-law officer visit and issue you a warning...We have ordered a trap for the cat and have taken pictures of the cat on our properties and will take you to court under the "cat running at large by-law."

Many of us have planted our flowers and vegetables and your cat has been digging them up. Every morning we go out to find our dirt messed up. We come home late at night to find your cat sleeping on our porch or messing in our gardens. This is very irresponsible of you....You have had a previous warning and yet nothing has been done, therefore we are going to take this situation further.

The letter was not signed. Even so, I couldn't let Terry take the neighbourhood wrath. "I'll go talk to her," I promised. "Maybe it's not our cat." However, I knew it could be as our cat hadn't used his litter box since the snow melted.

Fly, our previous cat, had also given us grief with the neighbourhood. That time I had avoided my neighbours and the problem. Since then Fly has eaten a Christmas ornament and died.

This time, I decided to face the dragon. That afternoon I captured Fly's successor, McFly, on my digital camera and strolled over to the home of the complaining neighbour. The whole area reeked of mothballs. I rang the door bell.

After several moments a young teenager answered.

"Are you the people complaining about a cat?" I asked.

"I'll get my mom."

He disappeared back into the house.

Several minutes later a woman came out.

"I understand you are having problems with a cat."

She nodded.

"Is this him?" I showed her the picture, hoping she wouldn't finger him. After all there were a number of cats continually roaming our neighbourhood. McFly has had up to five different friends visiting in a single day.

"Yes, that's him," she nodded.

My heart fell. She showed me her carefully tilled flowerbeds strewn with mothballs. The mothballs were intended to discourage our cat.

She told me how our cat had used her basement window-well as a litter box in the winter, causing a disgusting odour in the family room. She told me how he came by to do his business every morning at six, like clockwork. She told me how he would sit right up on her porch as if he belonged there.

"Not scared of anything."

I promised to try to keep him inside our house.

But with all the traffic at our home, this proved impossible. Several days later we had a bylaw control officer at our door with a stern warning about a $75 fine. We decided we had to find another home for McFly. Amanda and Elizabeth cried.

That weekend we took our cat to start a new life on Marty's sister's farm where he could have freedom and we could visit him once in a while.

If it is possible, as far as it depends on you, live at peace with everyone. (Romans 12:18)

Sometimes the Holy Spirit has to take me through circumstances more than once. I do want to be a good neighbour.

The Conversion of Mrs. Z.

Why I thought I could make a quick stop at Mrs. Z's house to pick up a prescription to have filled at the pharmacy for her, I'll never know. With this 87-year-old woman, just about every conversation turned into a lengthy affair as background and history were essential. Usually my eyes would glaze over, my mind would wander afield and invariably I would miss the point of the talk, which meant her starting over.

In spite of this, I liked Mrs. Z. We'd even had a few conversations about Jesus. She didn't see the need to ask Him into her heart as she didn't have any sins. I prayed she would be convicted.

On this particular day, I'd been out all morning. It was past lunchtime. I was hungry, but I had promised to pick up that prescription on my way home.

"Come in! Come in!"

First, she had to try her less than reliable blood pressure measuring device on me. "Sit here. Do this. No, no, bend this way...." I was at her mercy.

Then there was the package to wrap. Wrapping packages is something I know how to do. I may not be familiar with blood pressure gadgets, but I do own a heavy duty, sealing-tape dispenser. I've wrapped hundreds of packages. I know how to wrap a package. Mrs. Z had a roll of transparent packing tape. She wanted to tape a white sheet of paper with an address on it, to the top of a bulging cardboard box. She wanted me to turn the breadbox-sized box while she guided the tape. She was sure the tape would not stick to itself so wanted to guide it very carefully not to overlap. Impatiently I held the box, my stomach growling and eyes rolling, as she slowly, carefully steered the tape, directing me exactly how to cut each piece.

Suddenly she stopped. "Oh, I have to sit down," she said. "It's my blood pressure. Bring the box and the tape over to the couch and...."

I didn't wait for her to finish. I picked up the tape and quickly wound it around the entire box several times.

"No, no, no, not that way!" she waved her hands and whispered loudly with all the energy she could muster.

It was almost two o'clock. I was hungry. I wanted to go home. I stood up, put my hands on my hips, looked her straight in the eye and yelled, "Irene, I'm 51 years old. I know how to wrap a package."

She sank down onto the couch sobbing, "Oh Marian, will you pray for me? I feel so weak."

I looked at her and sighed, "And will you accept Jesus into your heart?"

"Yes," she said simply and plainly.

All my pent-up frustration evaporated. A big smile spread across my face.

"I've hurt you. I'm sorry. Can you forgive me?" she continued.

I led her in a simple prayer of repentance and a declaration of Jesus as Lord.

She gave me her prescription and I rushed out to the nearest drug store. "Thank you Lord! Thank you Lord!" I couldn't stop praising Him.

Fifteen minutes later, I burst into Mrs. Z's house with her pills. "Do you know what you just did?" I exclaimed.

She looked at me sheepishly from where she was kneeling on the floor beside the box, "I tried to do it myself." Her hand was taped to the box.

I cut her free and asked again, "Do you know what you did? You made Jesus the Lord of your life! You are going to heaven!

"You think so?"

"Yes!" I hugged her twice and left.

When he (the Holy Spirit) comes, he will convict the world of guilt in regard to sin and righteousness and judgment... (John 16:8)

The Holy Spirit does the convicting, but as His church, we have to do our part. He forgives us if we don't do it perfectly.

My Treasures?

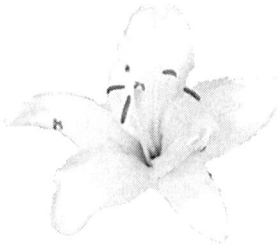

When Amanda decided to go on a retreat with her church youth group, Marty and I were more excited than she. This was what she needed. We lent the group our van, our cooler and a green plastic celery keeper filled with ice to keep the milk in the cooler cold. It didn't occur to me that these things might not be returned.

Several days later, Amanda came back, spiritually fortified. The van and the cooler were returned none the worse for wear, but the celery keeper had disappeared. No one on the trip had even the vaguest recollection of a solid green plastic container ideal for storing celery.

I looked at the wilted celery in my fridge and prayed for the keeper's return. Then I waited for God's design to unfold. Surely He had the celery keeper on its way back to me. Several weeks passed. I asked the head youth leader if she could perchance conjecture what could have happened. She said the group had borrowed two very similar coolers. My celery keeper could be in the other cooler.

I immediately asked the other cooler owner to check inside her cooler. She said she would get back to me.

The next time I saw her I found myself offering condolences as her cousin had died in a tragic accident. I just couldn't bring up my measly celery keeper. Then it dawned on me that I was spending a fair bit of energy, time, faith and prayer on getting back into my possession a $15 piece of plastic.

I recalled the dream the Lord had given me several years earlier, a dream that had helped me rearrange my priorities, but obviously they'd deranged since then. In the dream I had watched car after shiny new driverless car being dipped into a river. When I awoke, I realized I had been watching the baptism of cars. It was ridiculous—just as ridiculous as the earnestness of my prayers for the smooth running of our vehicles—especially when compared to my lack of energy and prayer directed toward winning my neighbours to Christ. In the eternal scheme of things which one mattered?

I stopped praying for the return of my celery keeper and tried to put at least as much desire into the prayers for my own brothers, who were brought up to know the Lord but had never asked Him to be the Lord of their lives.

Then one Sunday, at an after-the-service barbeque, I saw my celery keeper. It was full of serving spoons—but where was the lid? A celery keeper without a lid is not a celery keeper. I marched into the kitchen. I was on a mission. I looked into every cupboard, high and low.

In the middle of my search, my friend Dini came in, "Are you looking for something?"

"That's my celery keeper!" I pointed to the green plastic container full of serving spoons.

She looked at me sadly and shook her head. I had already told her my green plastic sob story, "No, afraid not, Marian. The church has had three celery keepers full of utensils for the last 15 years. Maybe you could put an announcement in the bulletin."

For where your treasure is, there your heart will be also. (Matthew 6:21)

O Lord, please give me this single-mindedness for things that matter eternally.

A Spotless Bride

The week after Steve asked Angela to marry him she bought an elegant, sleeveless, full bottom, wedding dress (off the rack to save money). The store which was out West (where Angela and Steve happened to be working at summer jobs) boxed the dress and sent it to our family's home in Ontario. When it came, I opened the box and admired Angela's taste, but wondered about the smudge marks on the bodice of the dress and the grit under the sleeves.

I phoned the bridal store in Edmonton voicing my concern. The lady there emphasized that Angela had received an exceptional deal on the dress simply because she had agreed to purchase "as is," stains and all.

"You won't really notice the dirt, but if you would like you could carefully spray a vinegar and water solution and sponge off any smudges. That's what we do in the store," she said. "But be careful, you don't want to leave water marks." I decided to consult Angela before attempting a delicate sponge job. I'm not known for a light touch. I had time; the wedding was still almost a year away.

Six months later when I laid out Elizabeth's newly-made white flower girl dress beside Angela's dress I knew we had to do something. The wedding dress looked grey and dirty.

At this point, there was no consulting Angela who was on a student exchange program in Egypt. She wouldn't be back until just before the wedding. It was up to me, the mother of the bride. I telephoned the local dry cleaners. They gave me a big price, no guarantees and an uneasy feeling. I prayed for wisdom.

Then I contacted a bridal-gown cleaning service. I explained my situation to the gentleman on the phone. He suggested I wash the dress myself. I was incredulous.

He assured me, "It's probably made of polyester. They all are these days. It's just plastic. You can't hurt it."

He told me to pick a sunny day with a slight breeze, fill the bathtub, add a mild soap and dip the dress in. After a good soak, I could swish the dress around and then lift it out on a heavy duty hanger. I could then take the dress outside, hang it in a breeze-way and spray it down with the garden hose. Sounded very straight forward and the price was right. I thanked him and hung up.

When I mentioned the plan to the family, they were skeptical, all except Elizabeth who volunteered to help.

Deliberately ignoring all my qualms, on a sunny, slightly breezy, spring day I filled the bathtub in our upstairs washroom with warm water and mild soap. True to her word Elizabeth was there to help. We plunged in the wedding dress with its several crinolines, pressing it down to soak.

Twenty minutes later we swished it up and down, and then I pulled the incredibly heavy gown up on a hanger. We let the water stream into the tub for a few minutes, and then Elizabeth held a large plastic bucket under the dress as I carried it downstairs and outside where we hung it on the awning support beam above the deck. Elizabeth and I took turns spraying the dress with a hose.

It dried spotlessly clean.

I telephoned the man at the gown cleaning service and thanked him profusely.

The cleaning of Angela's wedding gown makes me think of how God is cleaning His church. He gave us straight forward instructions in His Word and sent His Holy Spirit to guide us. Our job is to discern and obey.

> God said, "I am holy; you be holy." You call out to God for help and he helps—he's a good Father that way. But don't forget, he's also a responsible Father, and won't let

you get by with sloppy living. Your life is a journey you must travel with a deep consciousness of God. It cost God plenty to get you out of that dead-end, empty-headed life you grew up in. He paid with Christ's sacred blood, you know....

Now that you've cleaned up your lives by following the truth, love one another as if your lives depended on it. Your new life is not like your old life. Your old birth came from mortal sperm; your new birth comes from God's living Word. Just think: a life conceived by God himself! That's why the prophet said,

> *The old life is a grass life,*
> *its beauty as short-lived as wildflowers;*
> *Grass dries up, flowers droop,*
> *God's Word goes on and on forever.*
> *This is the Word that conceived the new life in you.*

(1 Peter 1:16–19a, 22–25, The Message)

About the Author

Marian den Boer resides in Hamilton, Ontario with her husband and two of her six children. Check her blog to find out more. She would appreciate hearing your "Blooming" thoughts and would welcome an invitation to speak to your group or organization.

Blog:
mariandenboer.blogspot.com

Email address:
marian@daviddenboer.ca

Printed in the United States
140401LV00005B/2/P